The Bimbo Has *MORE* Brains

Surviving Political Correctness

The Bimbo Has *MORE* Brains
Surviving Political Correctness

Cathy Burnham Martin

Quiet Thunder Publishing
Manchester, NH

QUIET
THUNDER
PUBLISHING

www.QTPublishing.com

This title and more are also featured at
www.GoodLiving123.com

The Bimbo Has *MORE* Brains
Surviving Political Correctness

Paperback edition: ISBN 978-1-939220-43-1
eBook edition: ISBN 978-1-939220-44-8
Audiobook edition: ISBN 978-1-939220-45-5

Published and printed in the United States of America.

Library of Congress Control Number:
2018932154

Dedication

I humbly dedicate this book to everyone who has served in our military, put themselves in harm's way, or paid the ultimate sacrifice…. so that the American freedoms we enjoy may prevail… including our right to peaceful dissention and disagreement with the powers that be. Those rights should never be taken for granted, for if we abuse them, we could lose them.

Thank you for your service. May we learn not to take any of our American rights and privileges for granted, for these are rights and privileges that are unheard of in many nations. We are so very blessed.

Thank you.

Other Titles
From Cathy Burnham Martin

The Bimbo Has Brains… and Other Freaky Facts

A Dangerous Book for Dogs: Train Your Humans

Dog Days in the Life of the Miles-Mannered Man

Healthy Thinking Habits: Seven Attitude Skills Simplified

Of the Same Blood: Your Eurasian Heritage

Sage, Thyme & Other Life Seasonings: Perspectives

Fifty Years of Fabulous Family Favorites, Volumes 1-3

Champagne! Facts, Fizz, Food & Fun

Boat Drinks

Dockside Dining: Round One

Dockside Dining: A Second Helping

Dockside Dining: Back for Thirds

Cranberry Cooking

Lobacious Lobster

The Communication Coach:
Business Communication Tips from the Pros

To see all books and audiobooks from Cathy Burnham Martin
go to <u>www.GoodLiving123.com</u>

Memoriam

On February 15, 2017, we lost my husband's first-born son. Christopher Martin, belovedly known to his friends as Spam, lost his long battle with opioid addiction. As with so many other addicts, Christopher struggled to even acknowledge that he was a user, never mind an abuser.

His family and dearest friends loved him through his years of addiction, always hoping that he could live through the day or night on which he would bottom out. Sadly, we lost this very loving, brilliant, creative man… far too soon. Such a waste.

Choices he made turned the world surreal for an amazingly large circle of friends. They'd laughed with him, partied with him, traveled with him, worked with him, celebrated with him, and, finally, wept openly as they mourned for him. We pray that the drug insanity of today will stop wreaking havoc on humanity sooner, rather than later.

Christopher… we all miss you and will love you always. Your laughter and passion for living will dance in our hearts forever.

Table of Contents

Introduction

The Bimbo Has _MORE_ Brains is for people who are sick and tired of being told how we "should" think and believe in order to be "Politically Correct." So, I will likely tick you off.... at least once. Perhaps many times. Yes, you may throw this book if so inspired. Just try not to hit someone else when you do.

We all get annoyed when someone ruffles our feathers or messes with our personal ideological comfort zones. For better or worse, we are mere humans.

A former boss of mine attended a 2017 Barnes & Noble book signing event for my original **The Bimbo Has Brains**. We'd chatted, I signed his books, and he left to cash out. Soon, however, he returned. We laughed aloud as he explained what had just transpired.

He'd handed the books to the cashier, who immediately announced that the author would be there soon to autograph her books. My friend said that I was already there, adding that I was super. (Thank you, Larry Gammon!) The cashier then leaned in, and he sincerely whispered, "But the title of her book isn't very politically correct!"

"She wouldn't have it any other way," came my friend's reply.

I'm so glad he came back to share the tidbit with me. That made me smile.

It's true. While I was raised to be polite, I do have a strong Taurus stubborn streak. I have especially never appreciated being told how I should think or feel about things.

As a great believer in "more than one right way to get things done," I soundly reject pushers of whatever "they" say that I "should" be thinking or saying or believing.

If we believe in what's "right" and true, can't we also believe in multiple ways of achieving it? If my thoughts don't pass muster with the "PC Police," I am glad. Push me, and I push back, thoughtfully and philosophically, if not verbally and actively. Tell me that I *can't* do something, and you can consider it *done*.

So, when I rallied for honest personal and professional relationships in **The Bimbo Has Brains**, I surely annoyed some folks. I was surprised to learn I was being called a powerful champion for women. Men also found the book enlightening, particularly due to the clarity delivered about what makes people tick, especially women. (We're not so mysterious after all.) Accolades from both men and women humbled me greatly. I'd merely meant to dash double standards, stomp on stereotypes, and help people understand each other better to improve the ways we relate to one another.

This time, we are causing trouble by reflecting on timely Life Lessons while ignoring political correctness. In fact, I am so fed up with political correctness, that I rather aptly dubbed it political quackiness. And we humans sure can be quacky!

I'll say it more than once. We seem far too hyper-sensitive these days. Everything can be and often is taken as an insult to all sensibilities. If you are a self-appointed member of the PC Police, you may prefer to stop reading now. Save yourself a lot of angst.

On the other hand, if you are sick of this age where people feel compelled to walk on eggshells and tip-toe around unpopular topics, then read on with great glee.

It's time to thrive, not just survive, in this world of forced political correctness. We'll be talking about sensitive topics, playing devil's advocate, and even riling up your sense of reality at times.

Life is true reality… actuality, if you will. I do not see real life in our age of "<u>un</u>reality TV."

If you feel at all the same way, **The Bimbo Has *MORE* Brains** is for you. We are the people who don't look at polls or tune in to mainstream opinion leaders to gauge our thoughts.

In that spirit, my approaches just may make you laugh… or quack you up. Some may even annoy you… or drop your jaw.

Through it all, I trust you'll find thought-provoking scenarios and crystal-clear reflections, as **The Bimbo Has *MORE* Brains** stirs your independent thinking.

Sit back and relax, or get ready to call your favorite PC Police. Simply dial Whine-One-One!

1
Attitude Check

> *"Women and cats will do as they please,*
> *and men and dogs should relax and get used to the idea."*
> -- Robert A. Heinlein (1907 – 1988)
> American Science Fiction Writer

I believe in living with passion, rather than shackled by political correctness. To do this with the most happiness, however, I learned that a good attitude makes the biggest difference.

Attitude is not a "given." It's something we each develop, whether we choose to develop a good or a bad attitude. We each have full control over our attitudes. But a good attitude doesn't necessarily come easily. The process involves something particularly difficult for us humans. It requires change. This change can happen at any time in our lives. Change can happen more than once... as many times as we need. Change can be inspired by a vast array of events.

For some perspective, I share the following true story.

* * * * * * * * * * *

Six little girls sat giggling at the small picnic table, celebrating one in the gaggle's 6th birthday. My friend, Marsha, the birthday girl, grinned with delight.

Lorraine Snay, her mother, had decorated the backyard pool deck with colorful streamers and balloons. She and her husband smiled as their little guests scarfed down birthday cake and ice cream. Party games followed, and then the pool party splashed into gear.

The littlest of the party guests laughed as she watched the others repeatedly leaping and diving off the diving board into the cool water. "Come on!" The others encouraged her more. "Try it!"

Splash! Into the water another one went. As they'd bob to the surface, they called out, "It's easy!"

The little one had held back because she'd never before seen a swimming pool, never mind a diving board. Obviously, it was lots of fun, so she finally scurried around to the diving board. Being such a tiny peanut, the board did not bend in the slightest as she made her big leap into the water.

Unfortunately, this little gal failed to surface. Needless to say, this party was finished.

Twelve years passed. Marsha and I were graduating from high school. Dr. and Mrs. Snay were sitting beside my parents. As I happened to be the class president, I had just addressed the attendees.

Lorraine Snay then turned to my mother and whispered, "We are so proud of Cathy. She has accomplished so much. National Honor Society, cheerleading captain, Student Council, Drama Club Best Actress, and New Hampshire's Junior Miss. Albert speaks of this often. He is especially proud, since he saved her life when she was a child."

My mother was perplexed to say the least. Dr. Snay wasn't even our family's doctor.

Lorraine explained to my mother what had happened at the birthday party so many years earlier. I'd gone off the diving board and hadn't come up. Thankfully, Marsha's father was there, acting as our life guard. He certainly never expected that he'd be jumping into the pool to fish a limp little girl off the bottom.

Being a doctor, he'd resuscitated me. When all was well, and I was breathing normally again, they'd driven me home. However, because I was okay, they hadn't mentioned it to my parents. That is, until this day twelve years later. Though this sounds peculiar, politically incorrect, and even crazy today, things were different in the 1950's.

When all the graduation festivities were over, my mother calmly said that she wanted to talk with me about something. Did I remember attending a birthday party at Marsha Snay's house back when we were little?

Of course, I did. Though Marsha and I had not stayed close, how could I forget being in a swimming pool for the first time?!?

My mother pressed for more information. She wanted me to tell her, specifically, what I remembered about the party. I reviewed the fun and food and activities, including the girls calling to me to come try the diving board. I clearly remember going to the diving board, but I have no memory of ever touching the water... or anything that happened after that.

Mom detailed what had happened and how Dr. Snay had saved my life. Wow! I needed to send him a BIG thank you!

So, what had happened? Did I drown or nearly drown, and he brought me back? Had I then simply blocked every bit of the trauma? I honestly do not know.

I do know that as a school girl, I suffered with a tremendous fear of the water. No one could understand why.

I'd been too small to start swimming lessons at the YWCA along with my friends. Back in the 1950's, you had to have grown to a specific height to be allowed to start classes. I was a runt. Once permitted to begin swimming classes, I clung tightly to the wall of the pool after every three or four strokes.

This went on for years. My parents were determined that their children were going to learn to swim. Quitting was not an option in my family.

Failure is just something that happens along the way to success.

My older sister was an absolute fish. My folks were not going to humor the idea that I would not persevere.

They were right. Ultimately, I became a strong swimmer. By the time I was in high school, I passed the Red Cross Junior Lifesaving course, followed by the Senior Lifesaving course.

I was still scared of the water, but I had learned how to push through my fears.

A lot had changed. I was no longer the runt... the classic late bloomer. I had grown up and become strong and determined.

When we gain the knowledge of the trauma that was likely the root of fear, we gain perspective. What we do with perspective directly affects our attitude and quality of life.

For me, perspective did not change my fear of the water. It changed how I <u>dealt</u> with my fear. I had knowledge. I had information. I had understanding, rather than just blind fear.

Change and perspective form the foundation for the Life Lessons shared in **The Bimbo Has *MORE* Brains**. As we gain knowledge and information, we can change and grow. We are not forced to do so, but we have that opportunity every single day.

We often hear stories of change that make us think. One is about two brothers who grew up in a single parent household in a very tough city neighborhood.

One brother analyzed his surroundings and circumstances, and every bit of information helped him grow to become stronger. He enjoyed a positive, fulfilling life, because he chose to use his difficult circumstances as a reason to do and be better.

The other brother blamed everyone else for his surroundings and circumstances, and every bit of information supported his need to grow increasingly angry. He dropped out of school, couldn't hold a job, abused drugs, got involved in a gang, and ended up in prison.

He'd chosen to use his difficult circumstances as an excuse to wallow and be miserable.

They had the same information. They had the same nature-nurture disadvantages. They chose to see Life from very different perspectives. This scenario happens far too often.

I try to remember stories like these and my own humble early story whenever I start to feel down on myself, my situation, or even our societal turmoil. These are the things that have taught me to live with passion, rather than political correctness. With passion I try to see and make each opportunity one of change… to change myself, my attitude, my behavior, my choices, and my perspective.

Say a little prayer. Tie a little knot in the rope. And hang on!

Tip:
> *"You can stand tall without standing on someone.*
> *You can be a victor without having victims."*
> -- Harriet Woods (1927 – 2007)
> American Politician & Activist

2
Role Modeling

"A lot of girls think they have to choose between being the smart geeky type or the beautiful bimbo."
-- Danica McKellar (1975 -)
American Actor, Mathematician, and Education Advocate

One of my common themes when speaking for groups of young people has long been helping them realize that who they are and how they behave matters and matters deeply.

Someone is watching, and they may well need us to be our very best. We shouldn't let others down, even if we don't realize that anyone may have been looking to us for direction.

Most of us feel too humble to recognize that we are worthy. And yet, we are setting examples for others with everything we do. Our words and actions are important. Whether we know it or not, we matter to other people.

We are all role models.
Our only choice is whether to be
a good one or a bad one.

This was brought home to me backstage at the 70th anniversary of the Miss New Hampshire Scholarship Pageant in 2016. They'd invited us "Forever" titlists (a nice way of saying former Miss New Hampshire titlists and far friendlier than "Has-Beens") to take part in the opening number as it flashed back through the decades.

Several of us were also involved in other parts of the production, through onstage contestant interviews, talent medleys, or chatting with the emcee. (That was my niche, as I had hosted the program for some 20 years.)

The Bimbo Has *MORE* Brains

Chatting with my Miss America Sorority sisters was both delightful and humbling. I had looked at each year's winner with admiration as the fields of contestants grew better and stronger with every passing year. Over the years, I had forgotten my own lessons. Someone was likely watching me, too, regardless of how unaware I was or how unworthy I felt.

One sister reminded me that she'd been just five years old when I was Miss New Hampshire. She'd kept my autographed photograph on her bulletin board, always reminding her that she, too, would follow in my footsteps and become Miss New Hampshire one day. Another said, "You always make me feel so good just by the way you talk to me."

The young lady who had been my immediate successor was there celebrating her 40th anniversary since receiving the crown. She pulled me aside and said she'd never forgotten the advice I gave her after she won the Miss New Hampshire Pageant. I'd said, "Don't worry. You'll get it right if you always remember to wear the crown in your heart, not just on your head." The advice had helped her many times since.

Several ladies said that I had always given the best pep talks to the group before each competition. They remembered that I never talked with them about myself or my accomplishments, but rather, I reminded them of how they were going to be so much better than I ever was… and why. One added, "I hear your voice to this day, and I know it's time to be my best."

One lovely lady gushed repeatedly about how I was her mentor and had made everything be about her and helping her to be her absolute best in Atlantic City and beyond.

They sent shivers through my heart with words like, "I grew up wanting to be just like you." I sincerely hoped I had truly been the lady they believed me to be. I prayed that I had not let any of them down with my own human foibles and faux pas. Remember the poem that advises us to "dance as if no one is watching?" I have my own spin.

Live as if everyone is watching.

Character may well be who we are in the dark, when no one is looking. But in broad daylight, bright spotlights, or full work lights, everyone can see the good, the bad, and the ugly about us. It takes daily work to remain calm, thoughtful, and responsive to life.

Regardless of how you may feel politically, I like it when politicians respond thoughtfully, regardless of how dramatically they may be getting grilled.

A good example was seen in January, 2017, with former 2016 Republican Presidential candidate Ben Carson. The pediatric neurosurgeon, originally from Detroit, Michigan, had been tapped by then President-elect Donald Trump to be Secretary of the Department of Housing and Urban Development.

During his confirmation hearings, Senator Elizabeth Warren repeatedly tried to twist Dr. Carson into slamming then President-elect Donald Trump. The Massachusetts Democrat wanted a promise that not one dime would ever benefit Donald Trump or any company linked to him or his family in any way. Ben Carson remained calm and repeatedly testified that he'd endeavor to not benefit *any* one person, but rather, he'd work to benefit *all* Americans.

He effectively chose to respond, not react.

It's far easier to see what happens around us and immediately and emotionally react to anything and everything. However, it's far more valuable and productive when we choose an active role and thoughtfully respond to others. This is a wonderful tool in becoming a better role model, rather than a divisive critic. To me, it's a lot like good sportsmanship. We choose to be good or bad sports both on and off a playing field.

Watching sports events, we see the most obvious signs of good and bad sportsmanship. I respect the NFL when referees eject players who have lost all sense of sport and good sportsmanship and punch at opponents or display other signs of heinous non-professionalism. If bad behavior by "Testosterone Toddlers" is tolerated, players get unnecessarily injured.

In fact, if I was making the rules, such behavior would get a player ejected from the game for the first offense. If they offended again, I would dock them for 3 additional games plus hit them with a 6-figure fine. Oh, and if this didn't curb thuggish behaviors, a third offense would carry a lifetime ban from the NFL. Ouch!

My husband, Ron, adds an even tougher twist. He says that if a dirty play causes injury to another player, the offending player must not only be ejected for that game, but he doesn't get to play again until the injured player also can play again. Woah. If they happen to be unable to ever play again, does this mean a lifetime ban for the offender also?

Remember the protests led by some NFL players at the start of the 2017 season? Sportsmanship, integrity, and teamwork meant walking a fine line. Fans and sponsors became embroiled in the divisive politicking. We desperately needed sanity to bring folks back together.

In late September, 2017, New England Patriots quarterback Tom Brady sent out an Instagram with a picture of him and teammate James White. He simply said, "Strength. Passion. Love. Brotherhood. Team. Unity. Commitment. Respect. Loyalty. Work."

Green Bay Packers quarterback, Aaron Rodgers sent out a similar message. They wanted everyone's eyes to stay focused on the game, not on the unrelated protests with players kneeling or signaling Black Power by raising a fist during the playing of the National Anthem.

Role Modeling

As did millions of sports fans, one of my girlfriends posted a very thoughtful statement on her Facebook page. Her concerns echoed the divisiveness of the protests. She also recognized the serious issues that players were actually trying to protest. Naturally, a flurry of pro and con comments followed from folks who read her post. These protests certainly stirred our passions. Reading each flurry of words, I felt sad.

Just like in politics, people with differing opinions attacked each other as the uninformed, uncaring, uncivilized, and unpatriotic ones. So many people seemed to be angrily pounding their own chests as if they were the only caring people on the side of "right."

While I rarely respond to such commentaries, hers had been quiet and thoughtful. I wanted to give her some endorsement for her approach, while also providing a little food for calmness as people batted opinions back and forth.

I wrote, "Sick of so many years of politics and politicians dividing people. On the other hand, when we protested something about our school, we held sit-ins at school. When work conditions are intolerable, we picket at job sites. Soooo, I ask why we feel we should protest racial oppression and police brutality at sports events? Ah, yes. Publicity. I think we can do better than this… and still get media attention. (Instead we got athletes joining the politicians and dividing people.) In this particular mess we are all right… and we are all wrong."

It's important, I believe, to approach those with varying opinions with respect. Presume they are logical-minded, compassionate people. Thus, we must conclude that they have solid reasons for their opinion. The same goes for those who see the facts from a completely different angle.

Tip:
"Life is 10% what happens to you and 90% how you respond to it."
-- Lou Holtz (1937 –)
NFL Coach

3
Educate Me

*"Watch, listen, and learn. You can't know it all yourself.
Anyone who thinks they do is destined for mediocrity."*
--Donald J. Trump (1946 -)
45th President of the United States

Homer: *Operator! Give me the number for 911!*
"The Simpsons" (Homer)

We all have those "brain cramp," "senior," or "bimbo" moments, whatever we choose to call them. As we detailed in **The Bimbo Has Brains**, "bimbo" is an Italian word that means "boy." Leave it to American "slanguage" to "kookify" a simple word and generate all sorts of controversy in the process. We all know both men and women that could be called "bimbos" at one point or another, and yet, all those "bimbos" do have brains.

Just how smart are we anyway? How smart do we need to be? The answers are different for everyone. We all may have known people we'd likely deem as "brilliant." Perhaps they are great thinkers. Or artists. Or poets. Or comedians. Or inventors. Or musicians. Or problem solvers. Or simply display a wit, sense, and IQ worthy of Mensa International.

We certainly don't have to be a member of Mensa to enjoy riddles and word twists. Here's a little beauty with no riddles involved, just common knowledge and basic information. You will find the answers at the end of the chapter. (No peeking until you've tried answering them all on your own first.)

"A Quiz for People Who Know Everything"

1. There's one "sport" in which neither the spectators nor the participants know the score or the leader until the contest ends. What is it?

2. What famous North American landmark is constantly moving backward?

3. Of all vegetables, only two can live to produce on their own for several growing seasons. All other vegetables must be replanted every year. What are the only two perennial vegetables?

4. Name the only sport in which the ball is always in possession of the team on defense, and the offensive team can score without touching the ball?

5. What fruit has its seeds on the outside?

6. In many liquor stores, you can buy pear brandy, with a real pear inside the bottle. The pear is whole and ripe, and the bottle is genuine; it hasn't been cut in any way. How did the pear get inside the bottle?

7. Only three words in standard English begin with the letters "dw." They are all common. Name two of them.

8. There are fourteen punctuation marks in English grammar. Can you name half of them?

9. Where are the lakes that are referred to in the "Los Angeles Lakers?"

10. There are seven ways a baseball player can legally reach first base without getting a hit. Taking a base on balls… a walk… is one way. Name the other six.

11. It's the only vegetable or fruit that is never sold frozen, canned, processed, cooked, or in any other form but fresh. What is it?

12. Name six or more things that you can wear on your feet that begin with the letter "S."

Again, the answers are at the end of the chapter. I hope you surprise yourself and get them all correct.

The Bimbo Has *MORE* Brains

When dealing with "smarts" I enjoy looking for a little humor. I always like it when smart people can laugh well, especially at themselves. That's endearing.

As a marketing and corporate communications geek, I also like developing means to accurately measure marketing efforts. Yet, I thoroughly understand that statistics can say whatever you want or need them to say.

One of my favorite joshing expressions is that 92.7% of all statistics are made up on the spot. Ah-hem!

I remember a television News Director arriving on the scene in the mid-1980's where I was working. Miles Resnick wanted to either relieve me of my duties as the Arts and Entertainment reporter or shift me into some other, more "newsworthy" specialty area.

I delivered what is called the "kicker" in television news. That is the "good news" story at the end of a newscast. He dug around and found a statistic that said less than 10% of viewers selected their news program based on the arts and entertainment coverage.

He figured I'd hang my head. Instead of it proving his point, I immediately responded, "That is awesome!!!"

Stunned, his jaw dropped. He asked, "Why would you say that?!?"

"Well," I continued. "I would have expected that NO one would choose their newscast viewing habits based on arts and entertainment. This is wonderful!"

As greatly as it annoyed him, our regular ratings numbers also proved that viewers liked our community-oriented, lifestyle and entertainment news stories and programs very much. They were truly watching through the entire newscast to see the story that would be delivered at the end. Despite viewers begging for my spot to appear earlier in the half hour, our smart General Manager kept me right at the end... to keep them hanging in there with us.

Though News Director Resnick did not believe I could sustain my energy for any half-hour program, the General Manager, David Zamichow, tested me out on an hour-long live special. That success launched me as anchor for a new, nightly half-hour news magazine which would lead into the regular news time slot at 6pm.

Almost immediately, the news magazine program was topping the main newscast's ratings. You can guess what happened next. Very quickly, they hired a new anchorman to team with me, and I was shifted to anchoring the early and late news. Though a lot of hard work was involved, it was great fun being part of a team that climbed from "worst to first" and kept the top ratings flying high.

Was I the best choice for the job? Who knows? To news purists, I must have surely seemed an unlikely choice. Sometimes news savvy wins. Sometimes experience wins. Sometimes presentation wins. Regardless, it's usually out of our control anyway.

As the saying goes, sometimes we're the bug; sometimes we're the windshield. I have been both. There's little point in getting all worked up in a lather over it. Life, with all its twists and turns, simply has to make us laugh. I truly believe that those who are happiest have learned to value the ride.

If you're lost in the woods and have no compass,
one option is to wait for Autumn.
The birds will fly South.

Another opportunity for smart thinking and measurable marketing arose while I worked for my husband's telecommunications company. This was before cell phones and VOIP had gained great popularity, and businesses relied on copper landlines.

One of the industries in which this company specialized was tourism. We could offer toll-free numbers to these companies for just a dollar a month. They then only paid for calls when they rang in to the company. Many of these companies were "mom and pop" operations, with very low profit margins, so this was a tremendous asset. Yet, I saw them blowing big money on things such as Yellow Page telephone book ads, which I believed were pretty passé for many industries, including theirs.

Why not measure exactly what ads or placements get actual results? For example, for $15 a month they could have 15 toll-free numbers.

"Put a different one in every place you advertise," was my advice. Even use different numbers on radio spots used in morning versus evening drive time. In a trade journal. In a brochure. In a related magazine. On their website. At highway rest stops. And so on.

Each month's phone bill would clearly show which placements generated calls, if any. For just $15 a month, they had very specific information that showed precisely how much business was coming from which sources.

People typically found that zero calls came from their Yellow Page ads. They learned exactly what marketing dollars were making sense for them. That gave them a value-added bonus they were certainly not accustomed to getting from their telephone company.

Was I super smart? No way. I just looked at the resources we were offering and applied them to the customers we served in a way that was a big win for both of us.

Artificial intelligence is nothing compared to natural stupidity.

Sometimes "smarts" is simply a matter of perspective. When we are objective, we can see situations differently. We can see more than one "right" way to accomplish goals.

When I close my mind, I close my thinking.

We all know people who think and say that they are very open-minded people. However, sometimes these are the very same people who have extremely closed minds. They do not think objectively, open-mindedly, or out of the box, so to speak.

For some perspective and levity on problem solving, I now defer to a joke shared with me by a dear friend, who happens to be Polish. Offense is not intended nor implied.

* * * * * * * * *

Milo and Stosh are standing on the 18th tee at their Polish Country Club. They are the final twosome in the Polish Country Club Championship and are tied for the lead. The 18th hole is a beautiful par four with a deep valley descending down to a dogleg right.

Both Milo and Stosh hit long, straight tee shots which disappear down into the valley. A short time later, the fore caddie appears at the top of the hill and announces that both balls are within 6 inches of each other. However, there is a problem. Both of the golf balls are Titleist #4s.

Milo and Stosh look at each other and realize that they had not informed each other as to what kind of ball they were playing, nor its number. They quickly descend into the valley and, sure enough, their two Titleist golf balls are right next to each at the bottom of the valley in the middle of the fairway.

Stosh looks at Milo and says, "We had better get a ruling from a tournament official to straighten this out."

Milo replies, "This is the Polish Country Club Championship, and we don't want to be disqualified for making a mistake and hitting the wrong ball."

Stosh agreed, saying, "After all, we are tied for the lead."

Soon after, a rules official appears and examines the two # 4 Titleist golf balls. He then looks up at Milo and Stosh and says, "Which one of you is playing the orange one?

The Bimbo Has *MORE* Brains

* * * * * * * * * *

Brains are awesome. Don't you wish everyone had one?

Okay, while I'm on the silly side, I may as well serve you up
another. Sometimes something cute and sassy arrives in an email
from friends. In the spirit of a David Letterman Top 10 List, here's a
light look at what were dubbed as "Actual Elementary School
Excuse Notes."

10. Jerry was at his grandmother's yesterday, and she did not bring
him to school because Jerry couldn't remember where the school
was.

9. Ronnie could not finish his work last night. He said his brain was
too tired from spelling.

8. Eric hurt his knee in a karate tournament over the weekend. He
won his age group, but was in too much pain to do his math
assignment.

7. Amy did not do her homework last night because we went out to
a party and did not get home until late. If she is still tired, please let
her sleep during recess time.

6. Henry stayed home because he had a stomach ache from eating
too much frosting.

5. It was my fault Mike did not do his math homework last night.
His pencil broke and we do not have a pencil sharpener at home.

4. Scott didn't practice last night because he lost his tooth in the
mouthpiece of his trumpet.

3. Diane was late on Wednesday. She fell asleep on the bus and was
taken back to the bus yard.

2. Cody was absent yesterday because we were out bowling until 2am.

And the number one "Actual Elementary School Excuse Note":
1. Tommy wasn't in school yesterday because he thought it was Saturday.

Some people think that life experience compensates for lack of brains.

Okay, thank you for your patience. Here are the answers to the quiz that opened this chapter.

1. The sport in which you don't know the leader or score until the contest ends is… Boxing.

2. The famous North American landmark that is constantly moving backward is… Niagara Falls. The rim wears down about 2½ feet each year due to the millions of gallons of water rushing over it every minute.

3. The only two perennial vegetables are… Asparagus and rhubarb.

4. The only sport where the offense scores without touching the ball is… baseball.

5. The fruit with its seeds on the outside is… the strawberry.

6. The pear got inside the bottle because… it grew inside the bottle. Bottles are placed over pear buds when they are small, and they are wired in place on the tree. After the whole growing season, when the pears are ripe, they are snipped off at the stems.

7. The only 3 common, standard English words that start with "dw" are… dwarf, dwell, and dwindle.

8. Did you come up with 7 English grammar punctuation marks? The total of 14 are… period, comma, colon, semicolon, dash, hyphen, apostrophe, question mark, exclamation point, quotation marks, brackets, parenthesis, braces, and ellipses.

9. The lakes referred to in the basketball team name "Los Angeles Lakers" are in... Minnesota. The team started out as the Minneapolis Lakers and kept the "Lakers" name when they moved west.

10. In addition to taking a base on balls, or a walk, to get a baseball player legally on first base without getting a hit... the batter could get hit by a pitch; there could be a passed ball; you could have catcher interference; the catcher could drop the third strike ball; there could be a fielder's choice; a player could be designated as a pinch runner.

11. The only vegetable sold only in its fresh form is... lettuce.

12. Among the 6 or more things you could wear on your feet that begin with the letter "S" are... shoes, socks, sandals, sneakers, slippers, skis, snowshoes, and stockings.

Tip:

Facts are meaningless.
You could use facts to prove anything that's even remotely true!
Homer in "The Simpsons"

4
R-E-S-P-E-C-T

*"Stick to driving a truck
because you're never going to make it as a singer."*

These words were said to 19-year-old Elvis Presley in May, 1954, by musician Eddie Bond after Elvis auditioned to sing in Eddie's new band. Bond turned him down, and had to watch Elvis Presley record a local hit record just a few months later. Then, it's said that Elvis Presley politely turned down an offer to sing in Eddie Bond's band. The sting assuredly deepened when Presley's January, 1956 release, "Heartbreak Hotel," climbed to #1, and shot Elvis to status as a nationwide sensation.

Of course, Bond wasn't trying to disrespect Presley when he turned him down. He simply didn't see the value in the raw, new talent.

We may all do that, unwittingly, from time to time. Someone may seek our advice, and we may fail to take the time to consider multiple possibilities… and potentials.

Respect is important to different people for different reasons, but we all need and deserve respect. This starts with consistently behaving and speaking in a manner in which we'd want to be treated ourselves.

Consider behaviors that you would call acceptable versus those that would be unacceptable. Think of tones of voice that are acceptable versus unacceptable. The same goes for faces we make and actions we take.

How would you react if someone politely asked for your help completing a task? Then again, how would you feel if that same someone instead commanded you to do the task… in a tone that sounded rude and demeaning? Ordering or demanding is not ever the respectful choice.

Though the best lessons in life are free, they can cost a lot.

I am not one to engage in man-bashing. However, I get a kick out of quotes that make us say, "Hmmm." For example, former White House senior staff member and U.S. Ambassador to Switzerland, Faith Whittlesey, born in 1939, is noted for saying, "Remember, Ginger Rogers did everything Fred Astaire did, but she did it backwards and in high heels."

That said, there are far too many societies in this world, and even cultures and sub-cultures within our own society, in which women are still barely considered second-class citizens and even personal property. No matter how someone was raised, or the social mores of their particular society, this is simply wrong.

Mohandas K. Gandhi (1869-1948), known as Mahatma, "the great-souled one" and the preeminent leader of the independence-movement in British-ruled India, spoke ground-breaking wisdom on the subject. "There is no occasion for women to consider themselves subordinate or inferior to men."

So, why do we still find so many people, women especially, in personal and professional relationships that sting with disrespect? Too many people, regardless of sex, faith, race, or beliefs, are not being treated with respect.

People who think or behave in disrespectful manners need to do much better!

Duh! If what I am doing, about to do, or contemplating doing would hurt my integrity or credibility, then it is wrong. Period.

Ignore misguided people who cling to the old, "What they don't know won't hurt them." Only those who've never been on the receiving end of such insensitive drivel can even <u>begin</u> to defend it. What a misguided person means to say is, "What they don't know won't hurt ME." It is clear that an offender's focus is purely self-centered. Anything else is false or shallow at best... and without logical defense.

We should never do to others what would hurt to have someone do to us. Hmmm... I hear tones of The Golden Rule ringing here.

On the other hand, every time we open our mouths, we risk insulting someone. This is particularly true in the age of hyper-political correctness.

That said, none of us should want to put our right to free speech ahead of being respectful. So, we naturally try our best to speak respectfully. However, we may often say words or use expressions that mean no harm whatsoever. Usually, those very words and expressions do not get misconstrued as disrespectful. Sometimes, however, someone takes great offense.

Let's start by presuming that we are not trying to be intolerant, insulting, upsetting, disrespectful, outmoded, or outdated in our speaking. Except in cases where a speaker absolutely intends to be mean, disrespectful, and nasty, I think we need to lighten up! We've gotten wayyy out of control in our "speech-slamming."

What happened to free speech? Or is free speech only permitted when it doesn't purport to offend the PC police? Who named "them" as being in charge of what is and what is not offensive and to whom?

Quite frankly, I am offended by people who challenge perfectly harmless expressions and words, many of which that have been used sometimes for centuries with absolutely no harm intended. I am tired of folks trying to shame people who use them in speaking.

Isn't it possible that we're in a phase of society in which we are just wayyy too easily offended? Of course, some people enjoy looking for things that could be deemed as offensive as a way to put down the person or people using them. Hmmm... now THAT is offensive, whether or not it's PC.

So, under the new "rules," we are supposed to condemn freedom of speech if it might hurt someone's feelings.

We've all heard many expressions that are now challenged. For instance, Americans are to be called U.S. Citizens.

The word Caucasian is a no-no. Well, quite frankly, it had come to infer "white people," even though when first used as one of the five proclaimed races in 1795, it included most of Europe, northern Africa, much of Asia, and India.

True Caucasians hail from the Caucasus Mountain region. This region is recognized as the area in Asia including Georgia, Armenia, and Azerbaijan. People from the region tend to have very olive skin, not white. My own Irish Grandmother was disowned by her Caucasian father when she married an Armenian, a true Caucasian. Oh, we humans are so challenging!

So, now is it better to call those formerly known as Caucasians, "white people," "whitish people," "semi-whitish people," "formerly white people," "European-American people," or some other non-inclusive jibberish? Seriously.

Here's another word whose acceptability has shifted over the years. Oriental. Being from the Orient used to mean you were Oriental. No one was offended. Who decided it was an offensive or insulting term? Someone said we should say Far Eastern. Then someone else decided we should say "Asian." So, must we get rid of our Oriental rugs now or just start calling them Asian rugs?

While we are on the race topic, I admit that I've lost track of what we "should" call people of African–American descent, and "acceptability" seems to vary from one person to the next. Negro is out. Colored is whacky. Africa may simply be where an ancestor lived. African-American only truly refers to people in the U.S.A. and is a misnomer since not all people from Africa are black. Black itself leaves out a full spectrum of skin tones. However, the NAACP (formed by a group of white people, by the way) has been noted as stating that the correct term is Black-American, but I doubt there are plans to change NAACP to NAABA.

Then… as with most of us in dramatically increasing numbers… we have many combinations of races. Some like to be referred to as having a mixed race. Others say interracial. Hip for the moment seems to be "dual heritage."

If the truth be known, most of us have dual heritages, or even multiple heritages. Why is this being made such a big deal now? And why does it typically seem to point to black and white heritages? I believe old, leftover guilt plays a big role. So, hit flush and move on, because I doubt you or even your parents were slave traders or slave keepers.

Sexism gets in on this act, also. My work used to get me called words like actress, comedienne, hostess, sales lady, and waitress. In the fourth grade I wanted to be an airline stewardess when I grew up. (Of course, that was before I had waited tables.)

Now I must be called an actor, comedian, host, salesperson, server, or airline attendant. Hmmm… so perhaps a snowman must now be called a snowperson.

Mankind must be referred to as Humanity. Expressions like "you guys" need to switch to "you folk," "you people," "you all," or "y'all." I grew up as a bit of a "tom boy." Excuse me. I meant to say that I was sometimes gender non-forming.

Queer became homosexual and is now "same sex." A dwarf shifted to a little person and now to vertically-challenged. I used to be called direct and straight-talking. Now I can simply say that I am PC-challenged.

I poke fun, but I do see a serious side. There are certainly situations and circumstances which help us become more sensitive.

I call on my experiences with Easter Seals telethon training here. Over the years, appropriate lingo changed a lot. While every state has an individual array of services offered, Easter Seals was founded in 1919 as the National Society for Crippled Children.

Times changed. Someone decided that noting a situation as "crippling" might be offensive or seen as a put-down, so we started talking about handicapped people. Then, fearing that we were negatively labeling people, it evolved into "people who have a handicap."

Not enough. That morphed into more specific expressions, such as "people who happen to be blind" or "people who happen to have cerebral palsy," etc. Then we realized that we didn't even want to think of anything as a handicap. In fact, we started observing that they were "handicapable." Now we prefer to say, "People who have special needs."

We no longer say someone is "wheel chair bound." They are not "bound" since a wheel chair gives them mobility. So, they became "people who happen to use a wheelchair."

We don't want anyone to feel victimized. A polio victim is now a polio survivor. A cancer patient is now a cancer survivor.

We don't live in a ghetto or low-income, inner-city area any longer. Now we think that being an Inner Urban resident sounds more pleasant. We mustn't insult a poor person nowadays. Instead we should refer to them as a person living below the poverty line. This means we mustn't refer to "the Peanut Gallery," because that's where we poor folks used to sit in theatres… in the upper balconies, the cheap seats.

To call someone a rich person is also a slam. They are merely a person with material wealth. And don't call someone "uppity." Some think that whether or not spoken, the intention is to follow the word with the evil "N" word. But "uppity blankity-blank" was never an expression I even heard before all the talk of speaking incorrectly. I naively thought that uppity meant snootily upper class, arrogant, snobbish, or hoity-toity. Go figure.

Thanks to all the attention being paid to political correctness, there are no more rednecks or hillbillies. We are now blessed with People of Regional Persuasions.

And, of course, we cannot tell Polish jokes, or Irish jokes, or French jokes, or jokes reflecting or naming any other nationality. We mustn't tell jokes that might insult any employment type either. So, no more lawyer jokes, or politician jokes, or construction worker jokes, or anything else. Religious jokes are now complete no-no's.

I would be remiss not to mention the obvious here. Naturally, "dumb blonde" or bimbo jokes are totally taboo.

We must no longer engage in brainstorming to develop ideas in groups. Someone said the word "brainstorm" could offend someone with epilepsy. Seriously.

Ah, but we are also no longer fat or obese. Yay! We are merely people of size. Um… Did anyone mention to the PC police that "size" is one of those relative words? Plainly, "size" can be small, medium, or large, just as quality can be high or low, good or bad.

Designations such as "Men" or "Women" also confuse some people. We now have Gender Neutral Bathroom options rather than a generic rest room.

We no longer have old people, elderly folks, or seniors. What, you say? Well, the PC police decided that "people of advanced age" sounds more respectful. Thank goodness. This must mean that I won't have to have any more Senior Moments.

We never again will have a bad hair day or fear being seen as unattractive. However, we may remain Aesthetically Challenged. (Can someone with an ugly attitude now be said to merely have an aesthetically-challenged attitude?)

I will not pretend to be able to keep up with all this. Problematic words and phrases are deemed so by whom?

Elites and academics have invaded our sense of normalcy and attacked our freedom of speech. A great example of this arrived in 2015, when the University of New Hampshire released a "Bias-Free Language Guide" for its students. Hmmm... how did students live without *that* for so many decades?

Anything we might say at any time might insult someone.

Let's be serious for a moment. Democrats are insulted by Republicans. Republicans are insulted by Democrats. As an independent, I insult devotees on both sides of the aisle. Oh, good. I do like to be an equal opportunity insulter.

We sneer down our noses at team names like the Washington Redskins. (My high school team was the Redskins, so I am rather fond of it, personally. Now they call themselves the Grizzlies, but I'll always be a Redskin.) We're not supposed to sit Indian-style anymore either. You must only sit cross-legged.

So, the indigenous people in the U.S.A. shouldn't be called Indians. It matters little whether the word developed from the word "indigenous" or from the notion that Christopher Columbus mistakenly thought he'd arrived in India. In Canada the word "Aboriginal" is used. We're told in the United States that we should say, "Native." Hmmm... I was born in the U.S.A., which makes me a native, too. However, I am a native, spelled without a capital "N."

I disagree that we are speaking with hidden bigotry. Even if every allegedly offensive word and phrase has an intentional slur in its origin, in the majority of cases, I don't see it playing out today.

So, if you ended up feeling cheated or on the losing end of a bad deal, did you get gypped? According to the Oxford Dictionary as far back as 1899, yes you did. However, the word has a peculiar background. It was most likely derived from the word "gypsy" which was erroneously applied to the nomadic Romani people in the Punjab region of India, because the Europeans initially thought they'd come from Egypt.

Old words often have some nasty origin. For example, I have heard British people say, "Oh, bugger!" In today's context, they are typically referring to something or someone who did something silly or foolish. In its literal sense, "bugger" refers to Bulgarians accused of being sodomites back in Medieval times. I doubt anyone is alive from then to take offense, but the old connotation remains on the books.

Plenty of verbal expressions that many people use quite commonly with totally harmless intentions are now said to be mocking people for whom English was not their first language. For example, when we say, "No can do" are we insulting Chinese immigrants from the late 1800's? Or does "Long time no see" poke fun at our indigenous Americans? I guess talking like the character Yoda in the "Star Wars" films is scrambling English and picking on anyone who speaks differently… though he's most beloved.

Finally, during the holiday season we can all get in hot water. I believe in offering a greeting that sends out the loving message you want, typically reflecting your own faith. So, if I say, "Merry Christmas," and the recipient happens to be Jewish, they are not apt to be insulted any more than when they say, "Happy Hannukah" to someone who happens to not be Jewish.

We should all feel totally comfortable sharing the greeting we choose. However, even saying, "Happy Holidays" is considered highly questionable these days. How *dare* you suggest that you want people to be happy!?!

Tip: Pretending to be trustworthy is the exact opposite of being trustworthy.

5
Piler versus Filer

> *Sometimes I think my brain is like the Bermuda Triangle...*
> *Information goes in but gets lost and is never found again.*

Do-It-Yourself and home improvement shows regularly emphasize designers and stagers tending toward minimalism. Smaller furniture and very few décor accessories (along with no personal clutter) show rooms in a home as larger, with a more spacious appearance. This is great when you are selling a property.

However, when we are actually living or working in a space, it becomes far more important for designers to be practical. That means not at all the same things for different people.

> *Learn from everyone, but never imitate anyone.*

Many years ago, I got a great example of this while helping to organize a new bank. My banking duties included being the Senior Vice President of Marketing, Investor Relations Officer, and Community Reinvestment Officer, but I also served as our interior designer. (Welcome to a start-up business.) As the designer, it was easy to accommodate the desired image, colors, and flow of the spaces, but I also needed a full understanding of work and storage spaces in our far-from-paperless society.

Further, I had observed some very real and very telling human tendencies in our initial organizational days. For example, our CEO organized his materials in piles... LOTS of piles. And, bless his heart, he knew what was where in each of those piles!

On the other hand, our CFO needed countless file folders for all his materials. I don't care if it was one piece of paper, it got its own folder if he deemed it necessary. So, he had LOTS of file drawers.

The two men had previously worked together as banking executives for many years, but that certainly did not mean their approach to their work was even closely related. In fact, neither of them would have been comfortable, nor would they have worked well, had they been forced to work in the same style as the other.

So, while the furniture we selected for their executive office suites looked very similar, what hid behind the fine wood-finished exteriors differed widely. One had many shelves for piling materials. However, the vast majority of these shelves could be hidden at a moment's notice by simply closing doors over them. The other office housed a seemingly endless supply of horizontal file drawers behind the beautiful wood finish. No one would have guessed that thousands of files lived there.

It should be no different in our residential spaces. Don't torture yourself with minimalism or a lack of cupboards, closets, and storage areas if you tend toward having a lot of items. On the other hand, restricting your storage options does force us to clean up and clear out the truly unneeded "stuff."

I am also not a big advocate of too many open shelves in kitchens... or offices, or wherever, for that matter. Though the "displays" may initially look lovely, they are extreme dust collectors. I have better things to do with my time than to be repeatedly dusting such areas. If you want to see what's behind cupboard doors, consider having some glass doors or just a few totally open areas.

Along those lines, also consider how you like to store your wardrobe items. Some folks like everything folded or rolled and placed in drawers. Ohers prefer open shelving or the closed shelving of an armoire. Still others prefer a wide variety of areas for hanging clothing. Many need a combination of storage types. Never let anyone tell you how you should or should not arrange and store your items. Do what works for *you*.

It's also time to list it. No, I'm not talking about real estate here. The lists to which I refer are those that keep my chaos organized. I wish I had one of those minds that organizes thoughts and memories in neat, easy-to-recover files, but I do not. As a teenager, I learned that I had far better luck if I wrote things down.

This applies to the way I learn things also. For example, in classes, I learned better when I wrote everything down, including things I wanted to remember from textbooks. I would also type up all the notes that I took in class, as well.

Of course, I still call it "typing," but since we now have computers, it's really "keying." I still do this. I write things down I want to remember. Then I key them into my computer. Just that process in itself, helps information register in my brain better.

The world is kooky enough without trying to remember every little thing. Most of us write a grocery list before we go to the store. Otherwise, we tend to buy things we may not have needed, and we tend to forget things that we actually need. I know I am not alone in writing down my grocery list in the order I will find things in the store. This makes shopping a breeze, without retracing steps or backtracking to aisles I've already passed by.

I always write down my "to do" lists in a similar fashion. After I make note of all the projects I need to do on a particular day, I then prioritize them. Top priority goes to the most difficult or the most imperative item or items on the list. Getting a big or vital project completed, always makes the rest of the list go more smoothly, whereas completing several smaller tasks but NOT the most important ones, leaves the big project looming over my head… along with the stress of the important work still left undone.

I once heard an expression that makes me smile when feeling stressed with too much on my "to do" list. It said something like, "Eat a toad first thing in the morning, and you will encounter nothing more disgusting the rest of the day." I interpreted it to mean that I will be happier if I start each day by accomplishing one of the toughest or least enjoyable things on my "to do" list.

On the other hand, a dear friend of mine, Kathy Andrews, has a saying that provides perspective and balance. She asks, "Are you living your list or living your life?" It's very true that we can get so wrapped up in the importance of our "to do" lists that we forget to live. Balance is a good thing.

I also believe in "to don't" lists. Knowing what you don't want to do is just as important as knowing what you want to do... or like to do. We see this as particularly helpful when selecting a college major, making career choices, or deciding on where to live.

Obviously, these are all just frivolous examples of things that make us different. Being different or living differently doesn't make anyone wrong... or right. This is as equally true of day-to-day variations as it is for major philosophical differences.

One of the greatest things about the United States of America is our ability to think and express freely. However, we have started to see an inordinate wave of effort to slam people who think differently. That is not the America we want.

If I repeatedly tried to stop you from expressing your beliefs, your opinions, or your philosophies that differed from mine, you would rightfully become displeased with me.

Chances are very good that you would become uncomfortable talking with me at all. I had already shown you that I was not interested in listening to your thoughts. I was openly diminishing their value. In actuality, I was only showing that I did not *want* those thoughts to have any value with *me*. Thus, I put them down, rather than listening.

If someone constantly "puts down" or scoffs at the way we think, we tend to stop openly sharing our thoughts with them.

That may well be something that Presidential candidate Donald Trump tapped into for millions of people who had felt their voice had been silenced. Things he said while campaigning were often politically incorrect, but they resonated with the public on many levels.

Even our institutions of higher learning got in on that act as part of the Donald Trump protest process. Some even started trying (and succeeding) in blocking or removing right-leaning speakers from appearing on their campuses. Left-leaning advocates thought this was fine, as it suited their own agendas. However, it smacked loudly of the very philosophies they claimed to be fighting against.

Fascism. Totalitarianism.
The restriction of free thinking and speaking.

Sorry academia. Your charge is to inspire, encourage, and to teach students *to* think. Our schools, colleges, and universities should not be in the business of directing students toward *what* they should think.

Nat Hentoff, a noted civil liberties advocate and jazz journalist, was very verbal in his concerns about this. For decades he spoke out against all attempts to suppress dissenting voices, often stirring the ire of his closest allies in the progressive camps. In 2004, Hentoff became the first-ever non-musician to be named a Jazz Master by the National Endowment for the Arts, but protecting American civil liberties was also his passion.

Before his passing in January, 2017, Nat Hentoff vocally expressed his dismay at college and university leaders for not encouraging open-minded, freedom of expression on campuses that were discouraging or even preventing conservative speakers and dialogue. Known for attacking political correctness, Hentoff did not like people trying to censor others just because they held differing views.

I get it. I'd heard a lot of talk about some extremists on the "right" who were suspected of wanting to squelch free speech. And yet, following the election of Donald Trump as President of the United States, we all watched intolerance of free speech rapidly swell into a hallmark of left-thinking activists. If you understand the Bill of Rights and what gives citizens of the United States our freedoms, you recognize that free speech intolerance should have no "seat at the table," as it is utterly destructive to our way of living.

> *"The strongest weapon against hateful speech is not repression.*
> *It is more speech."*
>
> -- Barack Obama (1961 -)
> 44th President of the United States

Shouting down voices that we don't care to hear does not take away the thoughts, feelings, or opinions they wanted to share. Expressing our anger or concerns by preventing comments from politicians we don't care for or agree with is utterly counter-productive... at best.

We can and should do better.

Our differences are far more important than whether we are "filers or pilers." Our differences give us balance.

Intolerance of our differences throws us off balance. There just may be a lot of right in what seems wrong and a lot of wrong in what seems right.

Tip: God gave us brains to work out problems. We should take care not to use our brains to create more problems.

6
<u>Higher Technology</u>

> *Loneliness is when you finally get an email,*
> *but it's from the newsgroup server.*

Don't spill your guts on sites like Facebook. Do use social media safely. For example, never say where or when you will be in some particular place... especially not vacations. At some point when you return, it is fine to put up pictures.

If you are married or in a serious relationship, keep some photos of you and your lover or spouse on your site. Be sure to tag them, so anyone searching for their name will find them.

That is not be a problem for anyone who is honest. The likes of Facebook provide fabulous channels to keep in touch with friends and family and reconnect with those with whom we've become disconnected over time. Of course, these social media channels are only fabulous for those in honest and true relationships.

> *I would like to know when someone unfriends me on Facebook,*
> *so I could like it.*

We regularly hear stories about someone cheating on their spouse and getting caught because the lover ended up finding them on Facebook and learning that they'd lied about being single. The typical response of the offender tends to be that they hate Facebook. Duh.

I have heard divorce lawyers comment that Facebook, not to even mention all the other social media outlets, now plays an evidentiary role in about 90% of divorces. This is especially true when one partner is playing around with a younger person. The lives and activities of Millennials and their successors fly freely all across the Internet. Yikes! No wonder cheaters try to mask their identities.

> *I'm not a Facebook page. You don't have to like me.*

People can learn virtually anything via the Internet these days. Beware! If a spouse doesn't want you on Facebook, it's probably NOT because he wishes to "protect" you. It's more likely that he's protecting himself from being discovered as "married" by some unsuspecting flirtation or affair.

> *"A child of five would understand this.*
> *Send someone to fetch a child of five."*
> -- Julius Henry "Groucho" Marx (1890 – 1977)
> American Comedian, Film and Television Star

Computer technology is such a huge part of our daily lives that we likely are unaware of just how involved we are with technology. Much of it happens seamlessly.

Our home office printer is soon to be running low on ink, and the printer notifies the supplier, and a refill cartridge is on its way to your house. We forgot to bring our grocery list as we left to run errands, and we can connect with the refrigerator to double-check inventories. We are heading home from a weekend away, and we use our smart phone to turn up or down the heat or air conditioning. We have cameras that enable us to check in on children, pets, or home security from anywhere.

Back in the day when computers filled massive rooms and buildings, people did not truly imagine just how small or powerful or practical they would quickly become. In fact, in 1977 Ken Olsen (1926 – 2011) said, *"There is no reason for any individual to have a computer in his home."* Ken Olsen was an American engineer and early computer pioneer and co-founder/CEO of Digital Equipment Corporation.

Even the great visionaries of one generation can appear short-sighted to future generations.

The Bimbo Has *MORE* Brains

So much of what makes us appear smart is a sassy combination of brains and wits. If we can't "think," it doesn't matter how much book learning we have absorbed. We won't know how to apply it.

Think about it this way. We hear about a television program being called a "quality show." Or perhaps someone tells you that some particular individual is a "quality person." What do statements such as these truly mean?

Look at the word "quality." Who says that it only reflects GOOD quality. The word "quality" in a phrase may actually refer to something being chintzy or shabby. Those are measurements of quality also, although they reflect BAD quality. We've mentioned this already.

The same goes for a word such as "class." This could mean Fourth Class just as easily as First Class.

Sometimes we gain clarity in a meaning from vocal tonality, which is tough to glean from the written word. If I smile and coo, "Ooooh, he is all class," you would likely pick up the positive intonation. On the other hand, if I scrunch my brow and scowl as I scoff, "Oh, yeah, he is all class," you are likely to read the sarcasm.

This is one of the reasons that social media faces communication challenges. Some people did not know, for example, that typing all in CAPITAL LETTERS INDICATED YELLING AT SOMEONE! Sometimes, a person may just be a bad typist. So many things we do have a learning curve... sometimes steep, sometimes easy.

"I never knew how ugly and how stupid we were until we had Twitter."
--Kellyanne Conway (1967 -)
Counselor to the 45th President of the United States

We get better with practice. I have found that if I just hang in there and patiently stick with some new technology application, I will get comfortable to the point where I will forget not being able to "get it."

But I surely do not want to "sound" as if I am yelling at someone by typing all capital letters. That would likely be highly annoying.

When volume levels go up, up, up, sanity seems to go down, down, down.

This is true in small scale scenarios also. We yell at people through tweets and Facebook posts.

Social media has become more like ANTI-social media.

Someone posts their happy thoughts, and they are met by a flurry of happy-faced and angry-faced emojis. We see the door opened for a torrential downpour of angry expressions from anyone who disagrees.

Anger seems to be all the rage... no pun intended.

Just as you likely have, I have read some social media postings and thought the writer to be uninformed, sadly misguided, or dramatically overwrought. However, no matter how I may disagree with their sentiments, I never once thought of feeling anger toward them. I never once thought of writing something nasty as a response to one of my friends. THAT would be most *un*friendly.

I've also made this same sort of observation in day-to-day life. For example, my husband has strong opinions. One of his best friends for decades also has strong opinions... 180 degrees in opposition. When the two of them get "discussing," I know it's time to leave the room. I don't care if they're talking politics, education, history, religion, or anything else. It's going to get ugly. Guaranteed.

I've tried playing mediator. I'd let "the boys" get to some juggernaut. Then I'd look up the facts and share with them. This became increasingly unpopular because "the facts" often made it look like I was siding with my husband. It wasn't my fault that the facts "sided" with my husband most of the time. Although, as his wife, perhaps I was simply finding facts that backed up his statements, while not drilling down to find contrary evidence.

Hearing their "discussion" one recent night, I cringed, though I'd long before retreated upstairs behind my closed door. Ron's friend kept screaming louder and louder, desperately trying to validate *his* viewpoint. This went on for far too long... as usual.

The hatred and venom roared, as though believing differently was against the law.

In the morning, I found little square sticky notes that his friend had stayed up and written for Ron's sake. There was no awareness nor acknowledgement of the one-sided screaming rant, never mind even a hint of apology.

I don't care how different opinions are. I care about how we treat each other, especially when we differ.

The notes merely expressed an extraordinary sense of feigned superiority and reeked of down-the-nose sarcasm. He'd even quoted Henry David Thoreau, saying it takes "more courage to stand up to a friend than an enemy."

Well, quote me: People who think screaming louder makes their way of thinking more valid and profound should think again! They merely sound mean, belligerent, and intolerant... at best.

Don't worry, computer. Even I go to sleep after 30 minutes of inactivity.

I remember getting my first home computer. My brother is very savvy and helped me order it and set it up. He even got me the biggest memory and storage available, assuring me that I'd never need more than that. (Laugh Out Loud! He helped me upgrade so many times since then that I lost track.)

However, when he set up my first computer, he tried to take my big ol' IBM Selectric typewriter away. I wailed, "I at least need to keep it for typing envelopes!"

Well, I was wrong about that and many other aspects of technology. That typewriter quickly became a space hog and dust collector. I eventually donated it to some mortgage loan officers who still needed it for their mega-paper world.

Higher technology in communication today typically refers to social media. I am not fond of people using this voice to hurt other people.

One friend had shared with her Facebook friends that she'd been diagnosed with bi-polar disorder. She acknowledged the challenges it had posed in her life. Then she felt deeply hurt when a response seemed to offhandedly dismiss her pain by telling her to simply accept that this diagnosis now defines who she is.

What? When has one aspect of any of us totally defined us? Like you, I think of myself as multi-faceted, but people can be so thoughtless and mean. This meanness spews so quickly and easily in keying in a response to someone's social media posting.

In this case, my friend was hurt and angry. I felt sad that she'd had someone try to slam her. I offered my comment, saying, "There is no law against ignorance. The best we can do is to keep educating people. Our challenges only 'define' us if we choose to let it be so, *not* because someone else states it. A person happens to be blind. Or happens to be bi-polar. Or happens to have cerebral palsy. Or whatever. Don't waste one drop of anger on ignorance."

Another friend had poured out his heart and soul and every resource he could to help a friend in need. That friend (or should I say "fiend") then walked away, saying, "Well, I never asked you to help me." My friend was floundering and said that he felt as if he'd been "hit in the stomach with a battering ram. What the hell happened?"

I replied to his pain-filled posting very simply. I said, "Sorry. Try not to let someone else's lemons sour your heart."

That's probably good advice for most of us at different times when we face some detractor slamming us for one reason or another. When someone else is being bitterly sour, we don't have to drink from their cup.

Not all put-downs are bullying. Some are just nasty-grams from naysayers and buffoons. When they use mass media or social media to spread their attacks to a wider audience, then it starts to smack of bullying. Cyber-bullying is hideously ugly and cowardly.

I offer one other perspective on the social media side of higher technology. The September, 2016 edition of Readers Digest featured the following quote from English comedian Ricky Gervais. "On Twitter, people sometimes say, 'Why don't you keep your opinions to yourself?' I go, 'YOU'RE following ME. I didn't tweet at you.' That's like going to a notice board in the middle of town, seeing a sign for guitar lessons, and yelling, 'I DON'T WANT GUITAR LESSONS!'"

Be kind. Devices and people both work better when we turn them on, not off.

Tip: Do not ever feel trivialized by someone else's opinions.

7
Economics

"I'll keep it short and sweet -- Family. Religion. Friendship. These are the three demons you must slay if you wish to succeed in business."
Mr. Burns (From "The Simpsons")

When I was born, $1 could buy you 24 pounds of potatoes or a pound of T-Bone steak or 1½ dozen eggs. Times change. Cost of goods changes. We work hard to attain a lifestyle that we want. It's not easy. Too often we can feel that we're on a treadmill, running hard but going nowhere.

Most people dream of not working and having lots of money. During an economic crisis 50% of those dreams come true.

Back in the 1980's, I came up with a nickname for some rampant overbuilding of condominiums in New Hampshire. What I called "Condomania" came from basic math.

If developers are building units at a faster rate than the population is growing, including both the birth rate and people moving into the area, something is very wrong. *That* is a bubble that is going to burst and take down a lot of people.

"Borrow money from pessimists -- they don't expect it back."
-- Steven Wright (1955 -)
American Comedian, Writer, and Film Producer

When the bursting bubble in the Northeast dealt a devastating economic blow to builders, bankers, developers, and real estate investors, many did not recover. People had been blinded by all the glorious cream on top, and just didn't believe it would collapse.

This Bimbo was among those who thought it was an industry completely out of control. When it crashed, those who had the same foresight and a lot of available cash, were able to capitalize big time by purchasing great properties at completely crazy rock bottom prices. Unfortunately, this Bimbo had no bucks.

We're not apt to see that again any time soon, because developers do less on speculation than was happening in the 1980's.

> ### *You only see that money is not the most important thing in life when you have it.*

Economics is more than just supply and demand. Savvy and smarts certainly help. That's illustrated in a little joke I heard once.

* * * * * * * * * * *

After finding a leak in the bathroom, the lawyer's secretary called the plumber, who fixed it in a matter of minutes. The bill, however, was substantial. The lawyer called to complain.

"You weren't here for more than 10 minutes," he said. "Even I don't charge that much for an hour."

"I know," replied the plumber sympathetically. "I didn't either... when I was a lawyer."

* * * * * * * * * * *

> *It doesn't matter how much you work,*
> *there will always be a jerk that works less but gets more.*

I know a family that made many millions of dollars. They did it the old-fashioned way. They earned it. They are solid, blue-collar folks and invested all their time into making their business work. And it worked... very well.

When they sold the company, all their family members for a couple generations could have simply retired and lived very comfortably. Instead, they started more companies, invested in local enterprises, grew businesses, and employed lots of other people.

Most importantly, they taught solid work ethic principles to the next generation.

Cousins, nephews, nieces, and everyone else related learned there would be no free ride. Everyone worked. Everyone benefited. Even when attending a bridal shower or a Christmas open house in their home, I observed adult relatives helping to park cars, teenage girls hanging up guests' coats, and pre-school children walking around with baskets of party favors for guests. They weren't just there for the party. They were there to help out with the party.

I couldn't help but recognize how vital their example is for all of us… for the nation even. They taught that no one should expect a handout. They taught that everyone was expected to work. Even the smallest effort mattered. Everyone doing what they can makes success happen. No free rides.

Nothing is guaranteed to be easy, but who wants nothing?

If we consumers get in trouble financially, our debt ceiling gets lowered, not raised. We must cut spending in ways we probably swore we would not. It forces us to balance our budgets. I think such thinking should be applied to our government, too.

To make it easier to accept the economic realities of our lives, a little levity is a good thing. Consider the following.

- I work to buy a car to go to work.
- Life is scary. At least our work salaries are funny.
- As a CEO of a newly established start-up I slept like a baby… waking up every two hours and crying.

- I have enough money for the rest of my life… as long as I don't need to buy anything.
- I'm in a relationship with my job, and it's complicated.
- Work until your bank account looks like a phone number.
- I need a 6-month vacation, twice a year.
- If you want to earn money with the help of Facebook, go into Settings, delete your account, and start working.

Also, please forget the theory that women and math don't mix. Thankfully, that old school of thought has been proven false over and over again.

> *"It's always good to be underestimated."*
> -- Donald J. Trump (1946 -)
> 45th President of the United States

Back in the day when my checkbooks were handled manually, I had no problem balancing them to the penny every month. Later, with automated technology and when handled by a man, every month brought a new and torturous nightmare to unravel. That is not to say that the man couldn't handle technology, by any means. It is a reflection that this great, time-saving approach to banking just wasn't yet all it was cracked up to be. (This sounds somewhat like the "paperless society" we started being promised decades ago. The paper piles still grow.)

Anyway, let me get back on the women and money theme. I recall an executive meeting at that new bank I mentioned in a previous chapter. I was listening to an intelligent group of 20- and 30-plus year bankers plan their strategies for growing the bank. They set very logical goals, except in one area.

My challenge was helping them see they had set an outrageously unrealistic goal for new deposit accounts. Several months earlier, deposit accounts had risen very rapidly.

The reason was one-fold. The executive team had chosen a special promotion to keep our bank offering one of the Top Five interest rates in the country for Certificates of Deposit.

This brought in large sums of what's called "hot money" from across the nation. However, this was a short-term strategy, and they had decided to no longer offer those attractive rates.

As these one-year instruments began maturing, the bankers had overlooked that all that "hot money" would be flying out the window to land in some other bank that was offering high interest.

Meanwhile, the new deposit goal for the next six months still included all that same "hot money" staying put in their bank. Oops.

Basic math tells us that if you have $10, but eight dollars of it is going away, your goal to reach $20 really starts at $2, not $10. Good thing they had their Bimbo there that day to bring them a wake-up call. That was likely my only financial "save," but it was important at the time.

Don't let a conclusion be simply the place where you got tired of thinking.

I was not as "banking smart" as they were in any way, but I was a bit more objective. I did not have the power to stop them from setting deliriously unrealistic goals, but I certainly could temper the scenario with a strong dash of "reality check." Thankfully, these were "bottom line" thinkers. They'd merely been caught in what I lovingly call "Bimbo Moments." We all have them.

Tip:
"If you're interested in 'balancing' work and pleasure, stop trying to balance them. Instead, make your work more pleasurable."
-- Donald J. Trump (1946 -)
45th President of the United States

8
<u>Lead, Follow, or Get Out of the Way</u>

> *"Vision is the art of seeing the invisible."*
> -- Jonathan Swift (1667 – 1745)
> Irish Satirist and Political Pamphleteer

Most of us have worked with or for some wonderful people. Unfortunately, most of us have also known scenarios where our boss may have made our work extremely challenging and unnecessarily so.

Often these negative folks seem to have what I would call "little minds." There are people, too often in managerial roles, who don't seem have the personal mental capacity to recognize that other people can actually think for themselves. Some may be micro-managers. Some may have "Little Man Syndrome." Others may be dedicated pessimists.

Some of these managers will smile to your face and even openly sing your praises… at the same time they know they have already processed paperwork to have you laid off or even fired.

Nothing is EVER their fault. Worse yet, they seem threatened by anyone and everyone who seems competent.

We don't have a lot of options when our boss or manager isn't also a good leader. Unfortunately, the two roles do not frequently go hand-in-hand.

We think we can see clearly, which is when we are most blind.

Those without sight often have far greater insight. Those with insight have greater vision than those who merely see.

Lead, Follow, or Get Out of the Way

I have been blessed to work with some tremendous leaders. They encourage us to strive to be our best… to be even better than they are. They inspire. They motivate. They empower.

"Don't tell people how to do things.
Tell them what to do and let them surprise you with their results."
--General George S. Patton Jr. (1885 – 1945)
Senior Officer in the United States Army

Many times over the years I have sung the praises of the best boss I ever had. David Zamichow was the General Manager at WMUR-TV when I did my first Easter Seals Telethon on his airwaves in March, 1983. From that telecast, my first time hosting anything on television, I was hired. He'd liked my style, my manner, and my voice. He certainly didn't like my resume when he saw it, as I had no broadcasting or journalism background. But he believed I could be trained.

"The greatest leader is not necessarily the one who does the greatest things.
He is the one that gets the people to do the greatest things."
--Ronald Reagan (1911 - 2004)
40th President of the United States

What made David Zamichow the best boss ever were many skills, traits, and approaches that I observed in him through the years that followed. He was frequently at the station first and stayed the latest. He listened. He took action. He took responsibility. He made things happen.

He inspired us to want to do our very best job possible. When we stumbled, we'd see that vein in his neck throbbing, but he'd be asking us if we could think of something that we could have done better or differently.

He laughed. He worked hard. He had vision. He empowered others. He dreamed. He set goals. He worked with us to make things happen. He left us all far better than when we started.

The Bimbo Has *MORE* Brains

*"If your actions inspire others to dream more, learn more,
do more and become more, you are a leader."*
-- John Quincy Adams (1767 – 1848)
6th President of the United States

We can consider ourselves lucky if we have a manager that does
even one of two of those things regularly.

I know. I've had the bad example types. One of my first bosses in a
big retail department store spent more time upstairs in the break
room playing cards with other managers than in our department. I
was sixteen years old. I knew I was not observing a good example.

Another boss was the owner and chef at a restaurant where I
worked during college. He kept us aware and on our toes, as we
never knew what he might be hurling across the kitchen when he
was angry at someone… which happened a lot. I neither speak nor
understand Greek, but I most assuredly knew when he was
swearing at someone.

Most bad example types are not that dramatic. Most bosses are
doing their very best. They are simply not leaders.

I enjoyed a boss I had while recruiting for a secretarial college in
Boston, Massachusetts. He'd treated us respectfully and made us
feel like part of his family. That is, until I got an unsolicited job
offer that would double my salary, recruiting students for a
competing college. I'd gone to him regarding the job, because I felt
flattered. As a young professional, this would be a tough offer to
reject, but I loved my job. In just one year, I'd enthusiastically led
the charge, taking them from one dormitory to five dormitories for
out-of-state students.

Unfortunately, this CEO didn't even discuss it with me. Instead, he
called me a liar, flat out, straight to my face!

I was shattered. I cried. I also quit and took the other job recruiting
away students that could have been his.

Lead, Follow, or Get Out of the Way

*"I am not afraid of an army of lions led by a sheep;
I am afraid of an army of sheep led by a lion."*
-- Alexander the Great (356-323 BC)
King of Macedon

This will sound mean and politically incorrect, but I felt no remorse to see that secretarial college enrollment crash, taking them back down to one dorm in one year and out of business in two.

And my new boss, the Dean of Admissions at New Hampshire College, now called Southern New Hampshire University, was marvelous. James Reynolds admitted to me that he'd had to create a job for me just to get me off the road for the other school. He needed to either hire me or drop three of the college's majors that I'd been devastating. Clever man.

Reynolds was also an inspirational, brilliant, influential, and fair-minded leader. He was a pace-setter and big thinker. He was a marvelous "we" versus "me" thinker. My kind of boss.

I have been blessed to have worked with many true leaders. It's awesome to learn from such greatness.

*"Nearly all men can stand adversity,
but if you want to test a man's character,
give him power."*
--Abraham Lincoln (1809-1865)
16th President of the United States

Years ago, I'd heard the expression, "Lead, follow, or get out of the way." While it sounds like a wise-crack, it contains much wisdom. Life is unnecessarily challenging when someone unqualified tries to lead or someone full of themselves doesn't know how to follow.

Yikes! As with most of us, I have stepped out of the way many times for someone better suited than I for a given role. I feel no slight in doing so.

*"What separates the winners from the losers
is how a person reacts to each new twist of fate."*
--Donald J. Trump (1946 -)
45th President of the United States

Decades ago someone related to me a very perceptive way of gauging someone's true character. Watch how they treat the receptionist at a company. Or how they interact with a janitor, a stock clerk, whatever. Look at the manner in which they handle relationships with someone on what may be considered the lower rung on the ladder.

This became very telling as we'd watch the flocks of political candidates sweep through New Hampshire for the Presidential Primary season every four years.

**How people interact with someone in a non-power position
gives a very clear guide to their true character.**

This observation has never let me down. There are those who believe they are somehow "better" than the rest of us. Their blood is blue... in their minds.

On that vein of thinking, I have had lots of people ask who was the best and worst Presidential candidates I ever met. There's little hesitation. Again, regardless of your political preferences, I am just speaking of people's character... via direct personal observations.

Some observations are simple. In Reverend Jesse Jackson's first bid for the Presidency, he glowed with charisma. The next time around, his charisma had vanished.

George H.W. Bush and his wife, Barbara, were truly wonderful people during campaigning and throughout their tenure in Washington. He was a marvelous mediator, and could manage to find common ground between people where there appeared to be none. She was one of the most beautifully honest and classy ladies I have ever met.

When Bill Clinton ran for President, his personality made him immediately stand out from the pack. His callously flirtatious manner, however, was annoying at best.

Candidates like Gary Hart and Bob Dole had wives that were easily superior to their husbands. Enough said on that.

Some candidates seemed nasty. Others seemed too nice. For example, interviewing George and Eleanor McGovern gave me the instant indication that he was far too kind and nice to be running for President. I am not saying the Democratic Senator from South Dakota was perfect, by any stretch of the imagination. I am saying that they both simply seemed too sweet for the swamp. Politics is a nasty business.

Then there was Tom Harkin, a U.S. Senator from Iowa, who made a bid for the Democratic nomination for President in 1992. While I didn't necessarily agree with all his policies or ideologies, I believe that the United States missed out when Harkin didn't get to the White House as President or as the Vice President when Bill Clinton got the Party's nomination and ultimately won the general election. Harkin struck me as one of the best ones that got away.

We also lost out by not getting the business savvy and leadership of Mitt Romney into the White House. On the other hand, he showed some very disappointing colors of annoyance during the 2016 race.

Those were some of the good ones that we missed. On the other hand, I met folks that seemed all wrong. The very nastiest person I met in politics comes down to a tie... a husband and wife team. Walter Mondale had been Vice-President with Jimmy Carter, but he had lost his re-election bid to Ronald Reagan in 1980. In 1984, Mondale returned to try to re-capture the White House, but lost dramatically to Ronald Reagan... again.

The Bimbo Has *MORE* Brains

Mondale and his wife, Joan, had made efforts to paint Ronald and Nancy Reagan as blue-blood, elitist Hollywood snobs. However, it was the Mondales that struck me as snobbish. Their public smiles and straight-shooting talk was dashed, in my opinion, when out of the public eye. I found them to be shockingly nasty and looking down their noses at everyone. The nation escaped a close one.

Oh, and by the way, the Reagans were lovely people who would have fit in comfortably at anyone's backyard barbeque. They were anything but snobbish. I also loved Ronald Reagan's knack at simplifying messages and delivering them with wit. He was inspirational and firm in his resolve.

> *"When you can't make them see the light, make them feel the heat."*
> -- Ronald Reagan (1911 – 2004)
> 40th President of the United States

The bottom line is that sometimes we elect leaders and sometimes managers. Sometimes we get good leaders, but other times the best we can say is, "Not so much."

However, just as in our own workplaces, we persevere. We do our jobs. And we hope they will do theirs… or quickly develop that ability.

> *"As it has for more than two Centuries, progress will come in fits and starts. It is not always a straight line. It's not always a smooth path."*
> -- Barack Obama (1961 -)
> 44th President of the United States

Another important aspect of leadership is accountability. This is true in our personal and business relationships. Accountability should be part of all aspects of life. Instead, we often find people rationalizing, justifying, or "passing the buck" by playing the blame game.

I am a big proponent of taking responsibility for what we do and decisions we make. When I managed other people, my rule of thumb was to give credit to them for things that went right and to take personal responsibility for things that went wrong. While many people saw this as risky for my own longevity, I found it a refreshingly simple way to get the job done right and earn respect from my team.

Applying this thinking to non-work scenarios is equally rewarding. Make a decision; make it yours; then make it right. This is one of my favorite philosophies. When I listen to people vacillate about any decision, this philosophy comes to mind. Wishy-washy, indecisive, or constant mind-changing appears out of control.

> "A genuine leader is not a searcher for consensus
> but a molder of consensus."
> -- Rev. Martin Luther King, Jr. (1929 - 1968)
> American Baptist Minister and Civil Rights Activist

My easiest fix for this is to start with good information. Weigh various sides of situations. <u>Make</u> decisions that best meet short-, medium-, or long-term goals and do not hurt or harm people.

Then comes a very important second step. Make the decision <u>yours</u>. This means not saying you did it because of outside influences or someone else's pressure on you. Claim the decision as having been made by you. Period.

To wrap it up smoothly, make the decision <u>right</u>. If certain action steps are necessary, then set up the needed plan and work your plan until you succeed.

Tip:
> "You have to think anyway, so why not think big?"
> -- Donald J. Trump (1946 -)
> 45th President of the United States

9
Coping with Being Hangry

Exercise?
I thought you said, "Extra fries!"

Sometimes we get angry because we have grown tired of someone hurting our feelings. Sometimes we feel angry because we feel out of control. Sometimes we feel "off our game" simply because we are hungry.

Have you ever felt less patient or a little irritable because you've been working like crazy and forgot to take time to eat? We get hungry. Or, in this case, we feel "hangry."

It's easy to relieve "hanger" pangs by eating something. If we feel "hangry" due to emotional or intellectual hunger, it can take longer.

But, as with most things, I believe we can relieve even philosophical "hanger" pangs by studying our perspective. When we look at things from a different angle and truly try to analyze the scenario with compassion for the person advocating it, our perception can change.

We may not change our own opinion, but we can get better at accepting differing opinions as being equally valid and fact-based. As is so often the case, it typically comes down to controlling our own emotions. These lessons bear repeating for all of us.

We live happier lives when we learn to thoughtfully respond rather than emotionally react.

In the last few years, I have observed lots of people reacting, especially through the media, if they have that sort of celebrity or access. Otherwise, we see it in ever-increasing volume over social media. The ranting and venting may serve as a personal release.

On the other hand, it definitely gets other people all riled up. It often makes them "hangry!"

What troubles me the most is not our widely differing opinions. I am troubled over the scathingly vicious manner in which people respond to friends who express views that differ from what someone else expected.

Call it "opinion-shaming" or "political-shaming" or anything else you'd like. It is unhealthy when we attack each other, even verbally.

Someone screeching at me or calling me names or putting me down for *my* thoughts certainly does not open my mind to *their* way of thinking.

Quite the opposite is true. When people express in purely negative or elitist or other airs of superiority, my stubborn streak starts to show. I do not want to be associated with negative garbage. If someone spews chaos and garbage attitudes at me, I do not get angry back at them. I simply have learned to accept it as an endorsement that *my* thinking is probably right on track.

Over the centuries, politics and unrest come and go. Sordid stories of man's continuing inhumanity to man remind us that we are not nearly as evolved as we would like to think. We need to learn to respond better as individuals if we, as a society, are ever to learn to do so.

Instead of jumping on whatever emotionally-inflated bandwagon is cruising by at the moment, I try to listen and look. Upon sorting through the hype, I usually can identify plenty of facts to validate both positions in a battle of wits.

What challenges me is the way I feel when I see someone on the receiving end of someone else's wrath. We can be so flipping intolerant.

Aargh! We want others to be tolerant of us. So, we must learn to show even more tolerance of them. To me, that is the only way to teach. Set the example. Be the change you want to see. Do even more than you expect others to do.

Kudos to celebrities like Nicole Kidman. Despite Hollywood backlash, she had the courage to speak an intelligent truth. Donald Trump was elected President, like it or not. He deserves everyone's support, just as does every other President. Duh!

Some screamed, "I don't like what she said, so now I will boycott Nicole Kidman." Fine. Go for it.

Here's a news flash. If we all felt that way, we would each need to live on our own little islands, because we'd end up trying to boycott everyone. There is absolutely no one with whom we will agree all the time. Heck, I even argue with myself from time to time.

When did civil disobedience become so uncivilized?

Even more importantly, why is civil discourse only okay if someone speaking out is in agreement with "my" opinion? There are better ways to get things done than screaming down those with whom we disagree. I especially like it when people who have the spotlight and microphone of celebrity use this power positively.

Actress Jennifer Garner showed her smarts as she took a positive approach to making her case. She is openly politically liberal and had not voted for Donald Trump. However, once he was elected President, she did not take to the streets or airways to protest. Garner took an active approach by lobbying leaders to rally support for her long-held cause… early education for poor rural children.

She then met with dozens of senior staff members on Capitol Hill. She even delivered the keynote speech to the National Governor's Association winter meeting.

The vast majority of the rural communities she regularly works hard to help voted heavily for Donald Trump. They did so based on his promises to make their lives better. Garner has seized the opportunity to continue working hard for people in struggling rural areas in her home state of West Virginia while holding President Trump accountable for those pledges.

Now that is first class all the way. I respect that tremendously. She is setting a positive example.

I respect everyone, including the many other celebrities, who stood up to the peer pressure they endured from those who were trying to "shame" them for their beliefs, words, or actions. We all should be allowed to express our beliefs without being attacked for them.

I also particularly respect the many professional athletes who have and are continuing to use their time and personal treasure to directly help their causes by becoming active in their communities. That resounds with good, old-fashioned American spirit and does great good without adding the divisiveness of fists thrust in the air or taking a knee during the playing of the National Anthem.

While I am just a regular "Joan Q. Citizen," lacking the visibility, spotlight, and microphone of celebrity, I try to pay attention to people who get attacked or bullied for their beliefs. This now happens so often in social media.

I try to come up with a response to let people know that there's light at the end of the tunnel, and it's not an oncoming train. I try to remind them that despite differing opinions, they are a miracle. They are worthy. They should not permit themselves to lose confidence in themselves just because others are calling them or their thoughts jerky or whacky or otherwise "wrong."

A friend of mine shared a message through social media recently. He said, "You are a beacon of light in these angry and confusing times. I applaud your courage. I admire your spirit."

He got me thinking. Aren't we all beacons of light for someone? Sometimes we don't even know. Sometimes, the news just makes us sad, confused, and even angry. Before she passed in 2001, my maternal grandmother frequently said, "There's just too much hate in the world." She was right.

We can do better. But it starts with each of us... as individuals.

We also need to stop putting it off as if we have all the time in the world. We don't. It's funny how we don't think about aging, until suddenly it happens.

I remember walking through a music store to get to the back where my videographer was setting up for a television interview. I passed by a couple young girls squabbling. One whined to the other, "Uh-huh! Paul McCartney was too in a band before Wings!"

Uh-huh, indeed! Of course, she could not name that band. But this was the mid-1980's. I quickly felt my age. We surely thought that no one would ever forget The Beatles.

That's all okay. There's nothing wrong with "feeling" even when it is difficult. Living life makes us feel. This is human. This is perhaps an important part of why we are here.

And then... we are gone.

Would people who'd ranted wish they could take back some of the bitterness if suddenly a friend or loved one to whom they'd expressed intolerance was suddenly gone? We often hear people express regrets for not having said, "I love you" enough or even "Good-bye" on a given day, and then the chance is gone forever.

Coping with Feeling Hangry

I do not believe the souls of the departed hold any ill-will. In fact, I believe they would want those still of this earth to love each other and be better to each other and use the wonderful memories as building blocks to do even better. I couldn't help but wonder what someone might say to those of us mourning their loss.

Then I got personal. I wondered what *I* might say if I was able to offer thoughts that could be shared after I am gone. I knew that I'd want to offer comfort to those who were sad. I knew I'd want to hear laughter from those who remembered how much I loved to laugh. I'd want them to sing and party and celebrate our times together.

What would *you* say? Or what list of things might you write down that someone could read aloud when you are gone. I gave it a try. Here's my list of things that, as the departed soul, I would like to say to all loved ones and friends left behind.

* * * * * * * * * * *

I have passed, but do not mourn… at least not for long. Celebrate my having lived and how you knew me.

Sure, I had unfinished projects. My Aunt June always called me the Queen of Unfinished Projects. Sure, I still had undone items on my "To Do" lists. I continually added more items. Sure, I still had unfinished books. I regularly kept 2, 3, or more works cranking at various stages of production. Sure, as on any day, I still had songs to sing, places I wanted to go, dreams I hoped to fulfill, and people's lives I hoped to somehow touch.

Life fed the fires of my passions, and I wouldn't have had it any other way. Through both good and challenging times, I am thankful that I always felt myself truly living.

Let's celebrate all the fun and adventures that we have enjoyed and shared… the dreams that have come true… the lives I hope I have touched positively.

I have been so blessed by great family, friends, and faith.

So have we all. Whoever we are... inside, and whatever we have done... outside, are blessings we often forget to count. However much we've loved and learned, played and pondered, I want you to be joyful.

So, while we may hope for a longer run on this ride called Life, it's relentlessly brief, even when we stretch it to 100+ years.

Our bodies decay. They crumble and die. But our spirits... our souls... they are not made of such fragile, time-sensitive materials. Have faith that we truly can and do shine forever.

So, miss me if you must. Feel sad that I will not again be able to look you in the eye, or reach out and hold your hand, or write more words to touch your heart. Or feel glad that we had our moments together on this Earth and be inspired to encourage others to stay so gleefully involved that they, too, will leave lots of unfinished projects.

Most importantly, be grateful to have left lots of people who feel and have felt loved.

Always know, we will all sing and shine together again. For now, enjoy being beacons for each other... some by shining the light... others by reflecting it.

Thank you for letting your light shine on me!

* * * * * * * * * * *

Tip: Go ahead. Try writing *your* message of hope and love for those we inevitably leave behind.

10
Evolve or Dissolve

Dream carefully, because dreams come true.

I'm old and old-fashioned in a great many ways. I studied to earn good grades. I worked to go through college. Even as a teenager, I didn't call in sick to work so I could join friends at the beach or to sleep in. I learned morals and work ethic. I worked two jobs... frequently. I grew up being very active in my Church. I volunteered in my community... constantly.

When I was young, I learned that if I blew my paycheck, I was broke until the next one. No, my parents were not going to pay for my foolishness. I didn't get into illegal drugs. I didn't get tattoos. I didn't litter. I didn't smoke. Friends have long quipped that if you look up "square" in the dictionary, my picture is still there.

I believe in the American Dream. I knew I wasn't apt to make a million dollars. But I knew I'd fight for your right to do so. Your RIGHT. I truly thought the American Dream was a sort of "right" in this country. Our parents worked hard so we could have a better life and a better chance for success. We worked hard to do the same for the next generation.

Hiccup!

Something happened along the way. The American Dream started slipping away. We thought that surely people would figure it out. Faith. Work ethic. Character. Compassion. So many great human traits would certainly prevail.

So, what happened? Entitlement thinking became a mainstream thought process. Aid was no longer thought of as a means to help someone get back on their feet. Or to help someone who truly couldn't help themselves. Assistance crept in as a highly lucrative "way of life" under the guise that it was simply milking the government. A callous denial developed to ignore the fact that working people are now having to increasingly support the lifestyles of those who refuse to work… those who have never put anything into the system by working, even though they were physically able.

"Leveling the playing field" stopped meaning everyone participating by the same rules. The American middle class was destined to slip to lower middle class with fewer opportunities to rise up into even upper middle class ranks.

Divisiveness and class warfare pitted Americans, even working Americans, against one another. Egregious lies and vicious fables started to take on "reality" lives of their own and actually won political elections. Lessons learned included, "Lie and cheat and people will celebrate your victory." Or consider this little gem. "Never mind when the facts get inanely manipulated."

One such expression that was frequently quipped within the news media was, "Don't let the facts get in the way of a good story." It was meant in jest, but sometimes, as we watch television, we can't help but wonder.

> *"As a nation, we don't promise equal outcomes, but we were founded on the idea everybody should have an equal opportunity to succeed."*
> -- Barack Obama (1961 -)
> 44th President of the United States

Then we wondered why the American Dream was becoming a distant memory. Government leaders seemed to no longer champion the opportunity for individuals to get ahead, since that meant getting ahead of the status quo. Our new generation of politicos sought to celebrate "average" rather than encouraging and rewarding excellence. I believe that caused far too many Americans to give up on opportunity.

While no one felt bad about helping those who *couldn't* work, annoyance grew over helping those who *wouldn't* work.

Do you remember the "47%" that Mitt Romney had referred to in his failed 2012 Presidential bid? This referred to the percentage of people not working or pitching into the system by paying taxes. What many did not understand is the fact that the 47% did NOT include retirees, or children, or any military families who are exempt from paying taxes during service. It reflected the growing numbers of people seeking a hand*out* rather than a hand *up*. This sounds down right depressing. They felt this was their *right* as Americans. Hmmm... just as I thought we had to right to work harder to earn a better life.

> *"The world is bad enough as it is;*
> *you've got no right to make it any worse."*
> --line spoken on the TV show "NCIS" by Jackson Gibbs, the
> character who was Jethro Gibbs' father

Differing opinions on how to do the right thing played a big role in making America strong. No one wants mass murder, homelessness, a weak economy, lousy or inaccessible education, unaffordable health care, or starving people anywhere.

However, these are all issues with multiple solutions and approaches to those solutions... all of which could be viewed as "right." That is why legislators need to be well-informed, open-minded, and able to negotiate and compromise. Each camp needs to be able and willing to give up some things they want to allow other sides to also get some of the things *they* want.

Only when BOTH sides can declare victory have we scored a victory for America.

Everyone walks away happy, and everyone walks away unhappy... with some things. That is how our forefathers created the Great American Dream. They did not agree on everything at any time in our history.

Disagreements among U.S. lawmakers are legendary. They span all generations, starting with whether or not to break away from Mother England and form our own nation.

Those disagreements continue to rage and span all issues. <u>That</u> is what's <u>good</u> in a two-party system. Dissention is part of a healthy system of checks and balances. No one person or no one party gets to have everything they want in every detail.

We, as people in America, have always enjoyed our right to hold and express our opinions. It makes me sad to see such raging anger expressed at people who happen to think differently.

I'll be the first to admit that I am stunned at some of the opinions held by some people I love… people I consider to be… otherwise… very smart. But I believe in their right to have a different opinion. (Or, as my husband says, "It's their right to be wrong.")

However, I'm not going to go scream at them, threaten them, or shoot at them, no matter how distasteful or even dangerous I think their stance is. They likely feel the same way about my opinion on the topic. Se la vi! Then we go have dinner together.

Yet, I do fear for the direction of our nation… the political climate our next generation gets dealt. Change is difficult for humans to accept. It always has been.

Something I'll talk about in more detail coming up is what I call Boomerang Bullying. This happens when an influential person or group calls someone out in a negative way, but the results actually end up going in the favor of the person being bullied. This is a fascinating and positive change I have been watching take root in the last couple of years.

In February, 2017, singer Joy Villa was scoffed at and put down openly by peers after she boldly wore a Trump-themed "Make America Great Again" glitzy gown on the red carpet of the 59th Annual Grammy Awards. Surprise! Her popularity skyrocketed, and her "I Make the Static" album leapt to the top of the best-seller list. She tweeted, "You either stand up for what you believe or fall for what you don't." She wouldn't be bullied into silence. The American public supported her strength.

Regularly, when elections or legislation has taken an unfavorable turn, I worry that it will be difficult, if not impossible, to get the Great American Dream back again. We must not stop believing.

I have no illusions of there being roads paved with gold or a true rags to riches story waiting for every American. I know that such Horatio Alger stories are both real and rare.

I feel blessed to have grown up in a simple, hard-working, blue-collar home. My parents made sure we all believed we could grow up to be anything we set our minds to... as long as we worked hard for it. I had no illusions nor delusions of grandeur. Recognizing that I would not likely ever become a millionaire, for example, didn't discourage me one bit. The opportunity is what's important.

It's the atmosphere, the economic and political environment that enables or prevents people getting ahead that's important. What we each do with opportunity is... and should be... highly individual.

Tip: We must first believe if we want to achieve.

11
<u>Bullies and Other Buffoons</u>

"It takes 20 years to build a reputation and 5 minutes to ruin it."
-- Peyton Manning (1976 -)
NFL Quarterback

What is wrong with us that we have allowed bullying to get so dramatically out of control... on all levels? Most of us can recall some incident or incidents from when we were children, and a bully was causing trouble for someone. At that time, however, parents stepped in, teachers had clout, community leaders fought back, and most young people rallied together to shut down the bullying.

Times have changed. Now we hear far too often about bullying in school getting so rampant that young people have taken their own lives to escape it. How do we prevent this? How do we not let bullying spin out of control?

There are always going to be nasty people... angry people... out of control people. Perhaps we can do better at teaching better behavior and communication skills to children. I fear that when we don't, the ill-advised behaviors become even more dramatic and dangerous as children grow older.

Little children who bully others become school students who bully. They become young adults who bully, spouses who bully, parents who bully, neighbors who bully, co-workers who bully, and more.

Bullies play on perceived or real power imbalances. They pick on people who may seem vulnerable. Aggressions can be expressed in many ways. Sometimes they use verbal attacks, emotional undoing, or physical violence. They can even bully by destroying your belongings or other property.

Now we also see bullying through social media or over cell phones. Cyber-bullying can ruin someone's reputation or self-esteem in mere minutes.

For decades, and even centuries, we have endured bullying against entire groups of people. Think about it. When our ancestors enslaved people in this country and all around the world, that can easily be called extreme bullying.

When women were denied the right to vote or work or be considered equal citizens in any way, that was also extreme bullying.

Though there are multiple interpretations of the Muslim Sharia law, the discrimination between how rules are applied to men versus women can be disturbing. The Muslim faith is far from the only religion to have oppressed or bullied women with discrimination. We see the same in all religions. However, many Western laws now protect women. Under Sharia law? Not so much.

For example, Sharia law permits beating one's wife if you feel she was disobedient. This is strictly against Western law, although it was not always so. If you look back at the old "blue laws" from the Colonial days in the U.S.A., you will find archaic allowances, such as it being legal to beat your wife as long as the rod used was no thicker than your thumb. Swell.

Under Sharia law women still lack rights in various areas, from divorce to rape. Women are basically deemed as inferior and lacking. Talk about a great example of mankind's outdated "man's law" syndrome.

> *"Every woman should be able to go about her day – to walk the streets or ride the bus – and be safe, and be treated with respect and dignity. She deserves that."*
>
> --Barack Obama (1961 -)
> 44th President of the United States

I couldn't help but be stunned when I saw a news story in 2017 about some young American women protesting in support of permitting Sharia law in America.

Freedom of religion is one thing. However, religious laws cannot be permitted that would go against the legal system. A simple example of that is in the fact the polygamy is outlawed in the U.S.A. So is murdering your own daughter or sister, despite how badly someone may feel dishonored by her.

Imagine the chaos if every faith could "insist" that their law must supersede State or National laws.

Everyone should be allowed to practice their faith, unless it breaks our laws. That is common sense.

Believe me when I tell you that I am not singling out Islam as the faith against women. However, by today's standards, it certainly stands out as not mirroring our common sense or values. Overall, Western society has been plenty evil against women from the get-go.

In Howard Zinn's book, "A People's History of the United States," he shares many examples of regular discrimination… or bullying… against women. One of them has been featured in various posters, publications, and websites, from Women's Day to the Washington Post. This list of rules hails from a time just before the Teachers League was formed to protest the automatic firing of any female teacher who became pregnant.

Let's look first at the 1872 Rules for Teachers. Per The Washington Post, let's examine the details.

1872 Rules for Teachers

- Teachers each day will fill lamps, clean chimneys.
- Each teacher will bring a bucket of water and a scuttle of coal for the day's session.
- Make your pens carefully. You may whittle nibs to the individual taste of the pupils.
- Men teachers may take one evening each week for courting purposes, or two evenings a week if they go to church regularly.
- After ten hours in school, the teachers may spend the remaining time reading the Bible or other good books.
- Women teachers who marry or engage in unseemly conduct will be dismissed.
- Every teacher should lay aside from each pay a goodly sum of his earnings for his benefit during his declining years so that he will not become a burden on society.
- Any teacher who smokes, uses liquor in any form, frequents pool or public halls, or gets shaved in a barber shop will give good reason to suspect his worth, intention, integrity and honesty.
- The teacher who performs his labor faithfully and without fault for five years will be given an increase of twenty-five cents per week in his pay, providing the Board of Education approves.
- You may ride in a buggy with a man, if the man is your father or your brother.

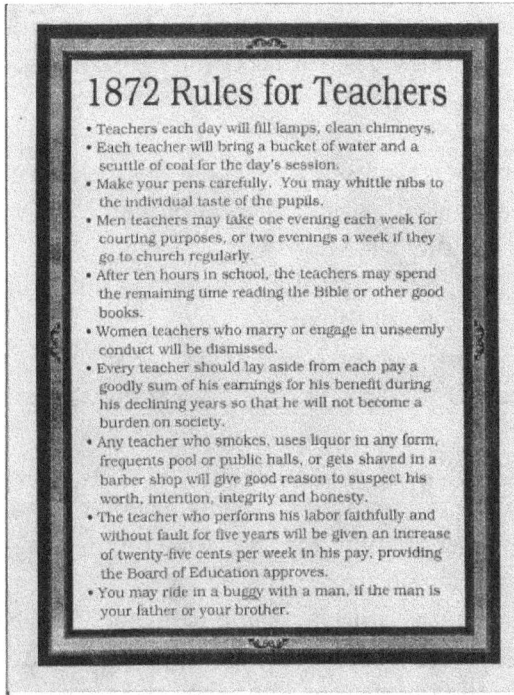

Male teachers could court, but they were only permitted to do so under rigidly limited conditions. Though men could marry, a female teacher was expected to remain a spinster or be immediately dismissed.

So much for separation of Church and State. Reading the Bible was openly encouraged as proper behavior once they'd put in their 10-hour day in the classroom.

I can also only imagine workers in any field agreeing to work for miniscule wages for a full five years, blemish free, in order to get a 25-cent per week raise. That's a grand total of $5.40 in 2018. And, of course, there were no "benefits" in 1872. I find it interesting that the teachers were encouraged to diligently put money aside for retirement, however. It was considered sad or shameful to have to accept monetary government handouts.

Today, far too many people feel "entitled" to such funds, as if the government had money that didn't come from the hard work of other people.

- Teachers each day will fill lamps, clean chimneys.
- Each teacher will bring a bucket of water and a scuttle of coal for the day's session.
- Make your pens carefully. You may whittle nibs to the individual taste of the pupils.
- Men teachers may take one evening each week for courting purposes, or two evenings a week if they go to church regularly.
- After ten hours in school, the teachers may spend the remaining time reading the Bible or other good books.
- Women teachers who marry or engage in unseemly conduct will be dismissed.
- Every teacher should lay aside from each pay a goodly sum of his earnings for his benefit during his declining years so that he will not become a burden on society.
- Any teacher who smokes, uses liquor in any form, frequents pool or public halls, or gets shaved in a barbershop will give good reason to suspect his worth, intention, integrity, and honesty.
- The teacher who performs his labor faithfully and without fault for five years will be given an increase of twenty-five cents per week in his pay, providing the Board of Education approves.
- You may ride in a buggy with a man if the man is your father or your brother.[1]

Then we can look at a 1923 Teachers Contract. Of course, by 1923, we'd made great social strides. Right? Okay, not so much.

1-https://www.washingtonpost.com/blogs/answer-sheet/post/rules-for-teachers-in-1872-no-marriage-for-women-or-barber-shops-for-men/2011/06/01/AGTSSpGH_blog.html?utm_term=.318226df7d2a accessed 12/16/17

Women were still chastised for behavior that found them taking a ride with a man other than their father or brother. Hmmm.... This is sadly reminiscent of a particular culture's practices nearly a century later.

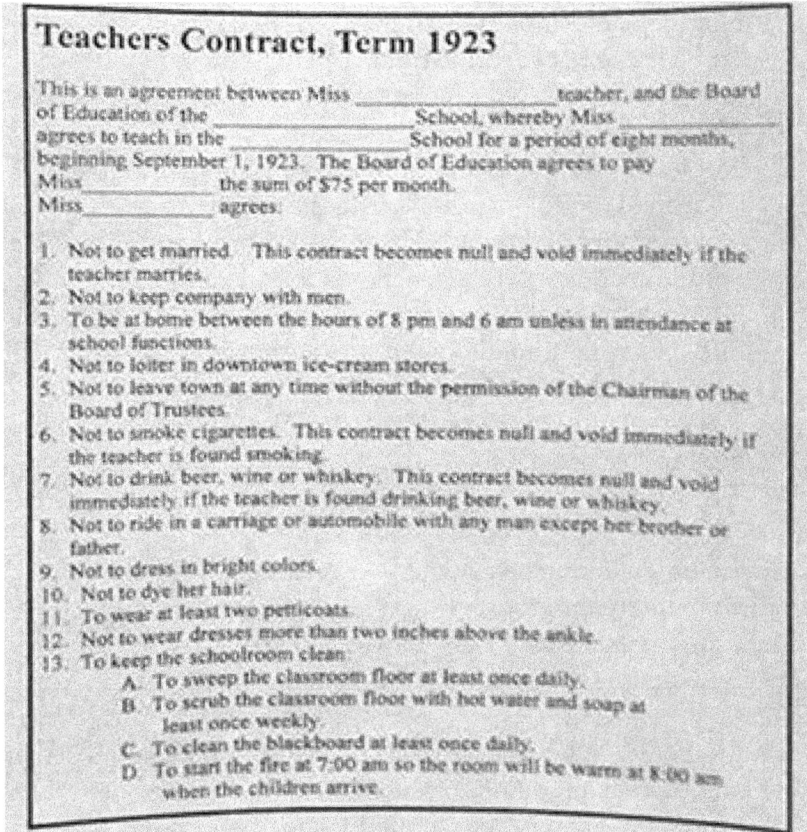

Teachers Contract, Term 1923

This is an agreement between Miss _____ teacher, and the Board of Education of the _____ School, whereby Miss _____ agrees to teach in the _____ School for a period of eight months, beginning September 1, 1923. The Board of Education agrees to pay Miss _____ the sum of $75 per month.

Miss _____ agrees:

1. Not to get married. This contract becomes null and void immediately if the teacher marries.
2. Not to keep company with men.
3. To be at home between the hours of 8 pm and 6 am unless in attendance at school functions.
4. Not to loiter in downtown ice-cream stores.
5. Not to leave town at any time without the permission of the Chairman of the Board of Trustees.
6. Not to smoke cigarettes. This contract becomes null and void immediately if the teacher is found smoking.
7. Not to drink beer, wine or whiskey. This contract becomes null and void immediately if the teacher is found drinking beer, wine or whiskey.
8. Not to ride in a carriage or automobile with any man except her brother or father.
9. Not to dress in bright colors.
10. Not to dye her hair.
11. To wear at least two petticoats.
12. Not to wear dresses more than two inches above the ankle.
13. To keep the schoolroom clean:
    A. To sweep the classroom floor at least once daily.
    B. To scrub the classroom floor with hot water and soap at least once weekly.
    C. To clean the blackboard at least once daily.
    D. To start the fire at 7:00 am so the room will be warm at 8:00 am when the children arrive.

While there is a photograph of this document, supplied via Woman's Day, which credited the Ohio Education Association, we'll spell it out long-hand here.

"This is an agreement between Miss ____ teacher, and the Board of Education of the ____ school, whereby Miss ____ agrees to teach in the ____ school for a period of eight months, beginning September 1, 1923. The Board of Education agrees to pay Miss ____ the sum of $75 per month.

"Miss ____ agrees:
1. Not to get married. This contract becomes null and void immediately if the teacher marries.
2. Not to keep company with men.
3. To be home between the hours of 8pm and 6am unless I attendance at school functions.
4. Not to loiter in downtown ice-cream stores.
5. Not to leave town at any time without the permission of the Chairman of the Board of Trustees.
6. Not to smoke cigarettes. This contract becomes null and void immediately if the teacher is found smoking.
7. Not to drink beer, wine, or whiskey. This contract becomes null and void immediately if the teacher is found drinking beer, wine, or whiskey.
8. Not to ride in a carriage or automobile with any man except her brother or father.[2]

It's easy to laugh at ourselves when we read such rules that are thankfully outdated in our society. However, these examples highlight practices that are now viewed as extreme bullying, perpetrated against huge groups of people.

Here's another twist for you. As all the celebrity sexual harassment and assault cases exploded into public view in 2017, we also learned that these practices had been tolerated for many decades. While they initially seemed centered in mass media and Hollywood inner circles, it was easy to recognize that such sexual bullying had been going on in virtually every sector of life, from politics to general business.

2- http://www.womansday.com/life/work-money/news/a40128/insane-teachers-contract/ accessed 12/16/17

I quickly started getting many questions from people wanting to know if I'd ever been victimized this way while working in the media. Blessedly, I did not see or experience this at any level during my time in television.

In all honesty, I did have one news anchor grab my leg one evening while I was on the news desk with the anchor team and introducing my story for that night. I kept a straight face, although I do not know how.

When my story started to air, and we were not "live" from the studio, I turned to him and told him in no uncertain terms that if he ever touched me again I would punch him on live television.

 He tried to laugh it off, saying, "Oh, you like it."

I said, "Really? Don't test me unless you are prepared for the circumstances."

He never touched me again. Female and male co-workers expressed full support and cheered my response. The young man in question was not long for that workplace.

I was fortunate. He was not someone in a position of influence over any of us. I didn't even have to involve management.

My heart aches when I hear of the great many people who abuse their power to abuse women in the workplace.

It is a very sick part of our society that men ever believed this was a proper way to behave. And it's sadder still that women so often feel powerless to overcome it.

They used to call it the "casting couch" in theatre. When I was a young woman I joined some theatre friends in New York City to go to some auditions. I performed in a showcase and received three job offers. Two were musical gigs, and one was a TV commercial.

The TV spot offered $50,000 up front, plus residuals, which sounded absolutely amazing for a day or two's work. That was more money than I'd ever made in two years combined!

Of course, I would need to complete an "interview" with an executive at the office building. I was told it would take two hours. The friend who was helping me acknowledged that this would be a casting couch. I would be expected to have sex with some man.

Nice. I politely refused the commercial "offer," and left New York City to itself. I did not seek stardom, nor did I want that or any other career that badly.

Sexual and other bullying is not just perpetrated by an individual or even any specific industry. Sadly, it still permeates all industries.

Extreme bullying is committed by groups, often very large groups. Our thinking and awareness is broadened now. Groups can and do gather to deliberately bully, as well. We have seen this via gang behavior for decades.

We have been increasingly observing it in many other venues as well. Group bullying is escalating out of control. This appears to be a direct result of our decreasing tolerance of different ideologies.

Consider the billowing chaos expressed following the 2016 Presidential election.

Toby Keith is one of the singers who performed at the 2017 Presidential Inauguration of Donald Trump. The backlash directed at the country star was sad. Faux-progressives, angry that Keith had refused to withdraw, then wanted him blocked from performing in a music festival in his own home state of Illinois.

They ranted that Toby Keith was "too political." To their credit, the concert producers refused to be bullied.

Several others, including Jennifer Holliday, were pressured to give up singing at the 2017 Presidential Inauguration... for no other reason than the fact that Donald Trump was being sworn in as President.

Wow! If I made somebody's short list and scored such an honored invitation, I would most assuredly expect my friends, co-workers, and peers to be honored for me and proud of me. My biggest cheerleaders!

If my theatre comrades, friends, and co-workers had pulled such a thing, I hope I would have had the courage to not cave. A once-in-a-lifetime opportunity to be part of one of the most precious parts of what makes America great had to be passed by... because Donald J. Trump was viewed as distasteful, at best.

That, my friend, is bullying. And buffoonery.

One of the greatest examples I saw of standing up to bullies came from the President of the historically black Talladega College. The school had been struggling to raise the $75,000 needed to cover travel, lodging, and other expenses involved in sending its 230 marching band members to Washington. Billy C. Hawkins appeared on "The O'Reilly Factor" on Fox News and shared their story.

Within 24 hours donations flooded their Go Fund Me site to the tune of $333,000. Within less than 2 weeks, nearly 8,000 donors, each giving mostly $5 and $20 contributions, had given the school nearly half a million dollars, enough to send the band and provide some much-needed scholarship funding, too.

Donor messages were loving, supportive, and strong. "Ignore the hatred" was the common theme.

The Bimbo Has *MORE* Brains

We humans are so very twisted sometimes. The people screaming that Donald Trump and his supporters were racists and haters, were spewing hatred in attempts to get their way. Do these people realize that *they* were coming across as hate-filled bullies?

Personally, I am glad Hawkins stood up to them and didn't allow hatred to deny his students the chance to enjoy a wonderful event. We all need to do a little looking in the mirror before we judge others.

We saw more of this during Senate Confirmation Hearings for President-Elect Trump's Cabinet. Democratic U.S. Senator Elizabeth Warren, from Massachusetts, repeatedly warned her Senate constituents that President Trump's cabinet choices had experience that should horrify them. *Horrify* them?

Hmmm... Has Elizabeth Warren not noticed that all her emotion and inflammation is horrifying? In truth, it's also embarrassing to me as an educated, hard-working woman.

Bi-partisanship seems to be a thing of the past. Party extremists on both sides are detriments to progress.

> *"There's not a liberal America and a conservative America.*
> *There's the United States of America."*
> -- Barack Obama (1961 -)
> 44th President of the United States

Do you remember when President Trump signed an Executive Order implementing a 90-day travel ban to give legislators time to develop legislation to better protect the nation from ill-intentioned people? I was mortified when I then watched some high school students in New York protesting against the ban... not because they were protesting, but because they couldn't even name the seven nations initially included in the ban. However, they were getting to cut class to protest. Some, in fact, were ditching a math exam. Nice priorities, especially when we realize that they didn't even know exactly what they were protesting.

When the reporter asked the protesters why they felt that vetting people coming into our nation was a problem, some explained that "only *non*-cool folks should be kept out." Then the reporter asked if they would want to see steps taken to only let "cool," friendly folks in and prevent the "non-cool," non-friendly-intentioned folks from coming into our nation. Yup. The students wanted that. Hmmm... They didn't grasp that it meant they actually agreed with Mr. Trump.

We forget that no one has any "right" to go to other countries. No one has the "right" to come to America if they are not Americans. It is a privilege, and the President of the United States has the right... actually, the duty... to keep people out who may pose a threat.

As citizens in the United States, we are blessed with the right to peaceful protest. I get concerned when I learn about academics leading their students down any particular path. These particular students were led into a protest that most of them did not even understand, and some of them joined just to skip a math exam. Hmmm... bullying can be so subtle, that we don't even realize we are being manipulated.

Most bullying is far from subtle.

We've heard and seen far too much in the open "shaming" arena of bullying. This started with people "fat shaming" or "body shaming" young women.

What right do I have to mock or slam someone as if they are less of a worthy person because their body is different than mine? Or that they should do something to change? We can be such nasty people.

"Los Angeles Times" columnist, David Horsey, does not have to behave nor write like a journalist, because he is not one. He is a columnist. This means that he writes opinion pieces about the events of the day or whatever else he chooses.

The Bimbo Has *MORE* Brains

On November 3, 2017, Brian Flood on Fox News reported on Horsey's column that fat-shamed White House Press Secretary, Sarah Sanders. Horsey had used the word "chunky." Of course, he had not used such descriptives in mentioning any *male* Press Secretaries, although there have certainly been some who could be observed as being over their optimum weight. Gee-whiz. THAT could apply to many of us!

Horsey revealed his own personal bias in scoffing that she looked more like a chunky soccer mom who should be serving cookies than a White House Press Secretary. Seriously?

Anyway, Horsey had further quipped that First Daughter Ivanka Trump and First Lady Melania Trump appear more to Trump's taste. What on earth would that have to do with the price of peanuts? Thank goodness that everyone in L.A. isn't sick-minded.

Hmmm... Did Horsey pick on Hillary Clinton's "body type" or for her wearing pant suits... though her husband, President Bill Clinton, had a very long and sordid reputation with "the ladies"... all who looked and dressed very differently than his First Lady? Of course not!

Horsey is just one of the gaggle that tries every possible angle to diminish President Donald Trump. In this controversial column he said that he envisions Trump would rather see, "Barbie dolls in short, tight skirts" at the regular press briefings than Sarah Sanders.

That's a fine way to refer to the Press Secretary. Sanders had been named one of the LA Time's "40 under 40" in 2010... as a "rising star in American politics." She is living up to the paper's 2010 accolades, despite lame attempts to slam her.

This is the "stuff" that gets me ticked. We use our own preferences to slam someone we don't like, as if our tastes or opinions are the only ones that matter.

It's too easy to jump on someone else's negative rant. "Well, everyone else is saying it."

I remember my parents retorting with some line of brilliance like, "Just because everyone else is saying it or doing it does not make it right. If everyone else is jumping off a cliff are you going to do it, too?"

So, when we hear people who don't like Donald Trump calling him things like a "sexually aggressive creep," it would be very easy to jump on the bandwagon. Bless their hearts, for as rough around the edges as he can seem, that sounds like name-calling for the sake of putting him down.

Blessedly, these people have apparently never met a true, sexually aggressive creep. Maybe they'd think a little differently had they experienced creepy or even questionable encounters with the likes of Harvey Weinstein or Matt Lauer or Bill Clinton... or perhaps... who knows? Thankfully, the LA Times had the perspicacity to remove all references to Sarah's appearance and got Horsey to issue an apology.

Ignore my ranting there. I am just wishing we would all step back for a minute and breathe. "Body-shaming" and "fat-shaming" seem to have digressed into "shaming" absolutely anything and everything someone is trying to put down.

In truth, because I don't like someone's criticism of me, it does not mean they are "shaming me."

On that note, we do not have to look to strangers or the media or the general public to feel the sting of personal criticism. It seems to be prevalent everywhere.

Too often we find people we know living quiet lives of struggle with their own partner or spouse. How we deal with lovers and other "stranglers" often colors how we feel about ourselves.

A shallow lover easily sees the physically beautiful and desires it all.
A forever lover discovers the beauty of the heart and soul within and seeks no further.

In the midst of the Monica Lewinsky White House sex scandal, a reporter asked the House Majority Leader if he would have resigned if he had been in President Bill Clinton's place. Dick Armey is said to have responded, "I would not have gotten a chance to resign. I would be laying in a pool of my own blood, hearing Mrs. Armey standing over me saying, 'How do I reload this damn thing?'"

-- US Representative Dick Armey (1940 -)
(R) Texas; House Majority Leader

Okay, these things are not the sort we need or want to joke about, but some levity, in my opinion, is better than screaming at each other. Everyone needs to remember when we say bad things or do bad things to someone else, it's wrong, no matter how justified we feel in our thinking or opinion.

How can our young people learn to behave any differently when we see adult leaders behaving so poorly? I have grown tired of watching supposedly mature, intelligent adults "go at it" like foolish children.

Do you recall the social media backlash after Donald Trump responded to Democratic U.S. Representative John Lewis? The Georgia Congressman had said that Donald Trump was an illegitimate President for destroying Hillary Clinton's campaign.

As ridiculous as that sounds, most people would just ignore it. Lewis spoke an untruth. Lewis looked foolish. Donald Trump should have left it alone.

However, Donald Trump seemed to either love the "fight" or chose not to carefully pick his fights. He put Lewis in the spotlight and likely *helped* Lewis when he told him to go back to his district and fix it.

Of course, Lewis couldn't leave it alone either. He made himself look more shallow when he responded with what turned out to be a lie. He tried to say that he would miss a Presidential inauguration for the first time since the 1980's... all because he refused to be there for Trump.

The truth is that he'd skipped a Bush inauguration, too. Okay, he doesn't like Republicans. He did not need to try to make it look as if his disdain was reserved only for Trump.

Here's a news flash for John Lewis. Donald Trump *is* your President, whether or not you like him.

To be an illegitimate President, Donald Trump would have had to have been ineligible to run or serve as President or he would have had to have won by ballot box tampering.

Those Congressional delegates who chose to jump on the "illegitimate President" band wagon should be ashamed. They knew better. They were contributing to unnecessary and harmful political divisiveness in our nation.

There are plenty of real issues that we should be protesting. I am weary of buffoons stirring up false ones.

And yet, opposing parties always make attempts to discredit leaders. You may recall people repeating, "Obama is really a Muslim." "Obama wasn't born in America."

Okay, now we have people saying, "Trump is really a misogynist." "Trump is a Fascist."

We need to grow up. We need elected officials to set the right examples for the next generation. The petty stuff has grown more than stale.

If we do a basic reality check, we all "get it" that both Liberals and Conservatives have members who are smart and dopey, wealthy and poor, Christian and non-Christian, men and women. Both Republicans and Democrats have Blacks and Whites, hawks and doves, practical and impractical thinkers, homeowners and homeless people. Both parties have folks who are lazy and hardworking, voters and nonvoters, aged and youthful, business owners and hourly workers. Why must we bicker and point fingers at each other... constantly?

We are used to "in God we trust" getting criticism. However, our Pledge of Allegiance is now surprising people for the wording: "And to the Republic for which it stands."

People are somehow just learning that we are a Republic. I did not skip Civics class.

Our Electoral College also came under attack following the Presidential election. Donald Trump earned 304 Electoral College votes to Hillary Clinton's 227 votes. That is decisive. And unsettling to many.

In hind-sight, many people then wished our system provided for a basic, simple majority election. With nearly 3 million more popular votes than Donald Trump, Hillary Clinton would have won. However, while she swept the West and Northeast, she missed middle America and the South. Clinton rocked Los Angeles, Chicago, and New York City, but she lost the nation's small towns.

One need not look too deeply into history to learn why our nation's Founding Fathers established the Electoral College. We cast our votes. Our Electoral College representatives then cast the votes to represent each region. The plan was literally set up to prevent rule by the masses... mob rule... the rabble... the crowds... the heavily populated cities... to ever be able to control the White House.

They believed that "mob rule" from the largest cities or concentrations of people would too easily squelch small cities and towns. They created the Electoral College as our system of checks and balances to prevent that from happening. It's important because the needs and wishes in cities are very different from the needs and wishes on a farm, for example.

Whether or not we liked the results, in the 2016 Presidential race we saw our Founding Fathers' foresight in practice. Otherwise, the heavily populated cities like New York City, Los Angles, and Chicago could have chosen the President, even though, combined, they represent only a fraction of the US land mass. Their economics, lifestyles, and needs tend to reflect huge differences from small town America, or farmers, or industrial centers, etc.

So, when our "side" loses an election, especially a hotly-contested election, it's understandable for the side that loses to feel grief and great sadness. We literally go through the traditional stages of mourning. Regardless of how strongly we want to cling to denial and anger, however, we are healthier if we let ourselves work through the process to acceptance.

To have Representative Lewis ranting that Donald Trump will never be "his" President and will never be a legitimate President just sounds childish. Donald Trump did not destroy Hillary's campaign. Even if he had, that wouldn't have made him less legitimate.

What I found most troubling was the revelation that whether a person was an FBI Director, the President-Elect, or a business person, if they disagreed with Democrats, liberals dubbed them as not legitimate, having no credibility, and called for boycotts. Nice open-mindedness.

This was an embarrassment, even to most Democrats. How can some people forget that just 8 short years ago, Republicans felt just as wretchedly saddened, concerned, and even frightened for the course of our nation when Barack Obama won. They feared for our military, our economy, our business environment, our health care, and much more. They didn't like the direction we seemed heading. They feared for the progress of our nation. They shared concerns and voiced them peacefully. They accepted the results of our election process and moved on.

However, some people have forgotten that many conservatives expressed parallel sentiments following the election of Barack Obama. "He stole the election. He's an illegitimate President. He's a racist. He's a bigot. He's arrogant. He's an elitist. He's evil. He's an extremist. He's totally self-centered. He has no experience. His inner circle is full of crazy extremists. He will ruin our country. Obama is not <u>my</u> President."

Another news flash. Obama was our President, just as Trump is the President for his dissenters.

However, one very large difference stands out in my mind. Republicans did not demonstrate, burn buildings, torture or beat Obama supporters, intimidate Obama supporters, or push for boycotts against liberal-owned businesses or Hollywood. There were no dramatic public speeches mourning the direction of the nation nor other divisive or hate-filled activities, such as blocking liberal speakers on college campuses.

Trump detractors even openly picked on, mocked, and bullied the First Lady. And the First Family. Somehow they saw it as acceptable to negatively imitate our new First Lady, Melania Trump. They endlessly criticized Donald Trump's children. They actually called for boycotts against Ivanka Trump, the President's daughter.

If Republicans *had* done any of this, Democrats would have cried out with scandal and outrage. And rightfully so. Our political two-party system has sadly become one of bullies and counter-bullies. All bullies and buffoons make me sick.

Tip: It's no good if we say that we are against bullying, if we bully.

12
<u>Great American Epidemic of the 21ˢᵗ Century</u>

I was very impressed to meet one particular man who literally lived the story of two brothers I mentioned in the first chapter. When I met him and he told me his story, I revealed that I was telling a parallel story in this, my upcoming book. He knew the story played out far too often in far too many families throughout our country, and he invited me to also share his very true story.

His name is Eddie Edwards. Hailing from a tough neighborhood in Atlanta, Georgia, Eddie's own father was a crack cocaine addict involved in illegal drug trade. Eddie focused on athletics and battled daily to avoid the gangs. His older brother lost that battle and now serves a lengthy prison sentence for a violent, drug-related crime.

Eddie credits his grandmother for teaching him values and how to make better choices. Eddie ended up serving in the U.S. Navy and graduating from the FBI National Academy in Quantico, Virginia. Navy service moved him to Portsmouth, New Hampshire 30 years ago, where the sincere, hard-working people he met reminded him of his grandmother's teachings. He knew he was "home."

Spending his career in law enforcement, Edwards particularly focused on substance abuse, which was near and dear to his heart. He remains a board member of the Partnership for a Drug-Free New Hampshire. Edwards says that it's time to "think differently about crime and punishment if we are ever to get a handle on our society's drug epidemic." He adds that "This is not a political right or left issue. It is about right and wrong."

Highly focused on fighting opioid abuse and tired of the waste in government, he became an early 2018 candidate for Congress in New Hampshire's First Congressional District.

My husband says that he doesn't think Granite Staters will vote for a black man. I give voters far more credit. They will vote for a good man of any color, and Eddie Edwards is definitely a great man. He may be a political outsider, not favored by the GOP mainstream, but if people meet him, they will vote for him.

Seeking to bring honesty and integrity to Washington, Eddie Edwards is raising his family with his wife, Cindy, in Dover, New Hampshire. If he wins, he will be a wonderful Congressman.

For me personally, I like his primary issue. Drug abuse is crushing us. When we lost my eldest stepson a year ago, my husband's grief was inconsolable. He struggled to get past questioning himself about what more he could possibly have done to have saved Christopher. Ron felt isolated, guilty, heartbroken.

I tried to explain that without shackling his adult son in our home, we were not in a position to change his choices. Multiple friend and family interventions had failed. Conversations fell on deaf ears.

Then, as my husband prepared to deliver the eulogy at his son's funeral, I tried to comfort him, reminding him that death was not Christopher's intention. He was a victim of what I'd been calling the Great American Epidemic of the 21st Century, affecting tens of thousands of families every year. We were not alone.

This is a behavioral epidemic. We need help... help that is above and beyond my pay grade.

Addicts have no concept that everyone around them can see right through them and their false bravado. They have no idea or concern that they are breaking the hearts of everyone who loves them. They only care about getting high.

It's easy for us to want to lash out, blame drug dealers, point fingers, and cry out for law enforcement to do something. However, there are no easy answers.

When someone is hell-bent on self-destruction, they can only change tracks when *they* decide they are ready.

We can get them food, housing, clothing, and health care. We cannot force otherwise smart people to make smarter choices. We cannot make someone accept help they insist they do not need.

Remember, to them, *we* are foolish, old-fashioned, stick-in-the-mud thinkers. *They* are the clever, creative, hip movers and shakers. They would be just fine, if we would all just leave them alone.

We try everything. Everything fails.

All we can do is hope and pray. And then, for far too many of us, the worst happens. Our loved one has overdosed. They are gone. There will be no second chances. They did not mean to kill themselves. They never thought they would not get another tomorrow.

Amidst the surrealism of grief and the tears from the hundreds of people who loved him, we very quickly learned that we were far from alone. Every family seems directly or indirectly touched by this tragedy. We all seem to know someone whose life was snuffed out too soon because of addiction.

It matters little if an addict struggles with heroine or prescription painkillers. The numbers in the U.S.A. alone are staggering. More than 20 million people a year struggle with opioid drug addiction. I've heard it said that a quarter of the people who try heroin develop an addiction. Yikes!

Drug overdose is now the leading cause of accidental death!

A 2017 report on a Blue Cross Blue Shield study revealed that opioid addiction had climbed nearly 500% in just the last 5 years. What?!? With those skyrocketing numbers, it's quite disheartening to learn that less than 1 in 10 addicts actually gets treatment for their opiate addiction. This is a very scary addiction.

The Bimbo Has *MORE* Brains

Three out of four opioid addicts didn't start with heroin at a party or out on the street. The majority of addicts started with prescription painkillers. Overdose issues from prescription painkillers alone account for an inordinate amount of emergency room visits, too.

The U.S. Centers for Disease Control reports that nearly 100 Americans die of opioid overdose every single day. Every day. These numbers are dramatically higher than deaths from guns or car accidents. 30 people a day are murdered by guns. 94 were killed in car accidents per day in 2016.

While all fifty states are now paying increasing attention to this drug crisis, we all need to be vigilant. For most of us this starts with gaining an awareness of how to identify when someone is using or abusing opiates.

There are signs we can actually see.
- A peculiar level of euphoria. Take note if your loved one seems oddly and overly happy.
- Drowsy with no logical reason. Do they seem sedated or lethargic?
- Do they seem to be passing out or repeatedly "nodding off?"
- Confusion or disorientation. For no particular reason, have they lost touch or seem mixed up?
- Look into their eyes. Normal pupils should not appear constricted or small.
- Watch their breathing. If it has slowed dramatically or becomes shallow, this is not normal.
- Are they suffering from dry mouth? Or constipation?

Other behavioral changes are also good indicators.
- Are they telling lies or being particularly deceptive?
- Do you find money or other valuables missing?
- Do they express hostility toward family or loved ones or try to transfer blame to others?
- Do they disappear, stop getting in touch, or avoid loved ones?

- Do they seem to withdraw from being with friends and family?
- Do they avoid making eye contact with you?
- Have they stopped expressing future goals or plans?
- Have they become unreliable at keeping commitments?

Remember also that not all addicts use needles. Don't be wooed into a false sense of security if you find no trace of needles or needle marks. A great many addicts never use needles. They can just as easily snort, smoke, or swallow their dope.

However, there are indicators we can see, if we look for them and put the puzzle pieces together.

- Skin quality is a fast indicator. Look for blotchy red patches or peeling, especially around the nose.
- Often there is dramatic weight loss. Any and all money is going to drugs; food becomes irrelevant.
- A runny nose is also an indicator. They may even complain that the air in the house seems too dry.
- Check skin for cuts or scratches that seem to have been self-inflicted, caused by scratching or picking.

We have a long way to go to get this pendulum to swing the other way. However, as ugly and painful as it is to think that a loved one may be an addict, it is far better to keep our eyes wide open. You are not alone. Reach out.

24 hours a day / 7 days a week / 365 days a year
Substance Abuse and Mental Health Services
Administration
National Hotline
1-800-662-HELP (4357)

Tip: If we can intervene, we might be able to save a life.

13
Police Brutality and Trutality

I have known a large number of people in law enforcement over my many years. Were they all perfect people? No. I do not know any perfect people in any field. Who does?

However, I can honestly say that the vast majority of people that I've known in law enforcement have been not just good, but wonderful people. They risk their lives daily. They leave their families each day or night with no assurance that situations from their regular work could cause them to never make it home again.

Unless we are serving in active military duty in a troubled hot spot, few other careers or jobs put individuals in such a challenging daily reality.

And yet, when something goes array, and police brutality looms its ugly head, it becomes terribly easy for a large number of people to cast aspersions on *all* law enforcement, rather than recognizing a particular individual or individuals as having acted horribly or rashly.

Personally, I cannot imagine having to work every day in some neighborhood where surviving violent crime has become a way of regular life.

Imagine trying to raise a child in such an environment. Imagine recognizing that many illegal guns and various other weapons are on many of the people you must walk past each day to go to work or to the store for food. Imagine the negative stress levels of regularly hearing yelling, fighting, police sirens, and even gunfire, while trying to live your life sanely within your home or sleep at night.

Whether in a large city or a small town, our law enforcement officials have chosen to serve to help make life safer for everyone. This is not an easy task. There is no officer who will do absolutely everything absolutely right every day.

However, we all lose when an incident of police brutality escalates in people's perception and reaction into an issue reflecting *all* police or even the majority of people working in law enforcement.

Remember, we humans are easily persuaded to perceive things in a slanted way. In preparation for Donald Trump's Presidential Inauguration, the American Civil Liberties Union directly influenced people to increasingly distrust law enforcement officials. Police presence would be heightened for the event, with hundreds of thousands of extra people in Washington, DC. The ACLU told protestors who were planning to attend to be sure to video all the police they could and to go ahead and get in their faces with video rolling. At the same time, they told the police that it would be interfering with people's personal rights for them to wear their body cameras during the protests. Hmmm.

Wasn't the idea to keep everyone safe? Or were they trying to protect activists who wanted to destroy personal property and harass other people without worry that the police would be able to track them down and identify them from video images?

To say that this smacked of hypocrisy is an understatement.

These were not the folks planning peaceful, law-protected protests. These were groups who were calling for violent disruption and "gleeful" anarchy.

They wanted to use the right to peaceful protest to keep police video away from some very evil, anti-American activity planned against fellow Americans. Nice.

They showed no concern for the rights of the millions of Americans who were *not* hard-left extremists or into any sort of radicalism. What about *their* rights? Ah, their opinions were not considered valid because they were probably bigots, fascists, rednecks, and other Trump supporters.

These were not people concerned with police brutality. These were not folks concerned with racism.

People have become equally enraged when a black police officer has shot a black assailant as when the officer has been white. However, since 2010 or so, it certainly appears that violent pushback has only become "the norm" when a white officer has, for example, shot a black suspect.

I don't get it. If I *say* that I don't want violence, then what am I actually *doing* if I respond with violence to something that upsets me? I am saying that *my* violence is justified. *Mine* was a response. *Mine* was to make a valid point.

Hello! There is *no* thought involved. There appears to be only hatred, ignorance, and distrust.

Think about it. What if the involved, offending police officer felt that same way? What if *their* use of force was in response to a suspect's behavior?

They regularly serve in dangerous situations, especially in cities. Perhaps it is even more stressful in Small Town, America, because law enforcement officials are less accustomed to deadly citizen violence, and officials might be more apt to be caught off guard.

I believe our law enforcement officials are protecting our lives. They often are risking their own lives to do so.

Let's look at crimes against Blacks in the same, highly volatile cities and neighborhoods that have become the most dangerous for everyone, not just police. For example, 2015 public records show more than 3,000 shootings a year in Chicago alone. Nearly all Blacks who are shot there are shot by other Blacks.

Whites are not typically found going into black neighborhoods to commit crimes or shoot people. Blacks are doing this in their own neighborhoods.

This isn't a White against Black racial issue. This is a human issue. Often, this is also an illegal drug issue, but that's another topic altogether.

God help the people who live in these troubled neighborhoods. God help the people who work there. God help the police who serve there.

And now, we add to this hatred-filled environment, the sick wishes of misguided people literally chanting and championing a desire to kill police.

What on earth??!!? What are we doing? What *are* we thinking?

We have not only lost perspective; we've lost our minds. We will cause our own self-destruction as a society.

Tip:

"Numbers have a way of taking a man by the hand
and leading him down the path of reason."
-- Pythagoras (570 BC – 500 BC)
Greek Philosopher

14
Bimbo Basics

> *"Every man takes the limits of his own field of vision*
> *for the limits of the world."*
> -- Arthur Schopenhauer (1788-1860)
> German Philosopher

I call our limited field of vision "Center of the Universe" thinking. As Americans, we tend to do this... a lot. We speak English and think everyone should accommodate us.

Yet at the same time, we provide interpreters for dozens of languages in our schools and public offices, rather than teaching English to our immigrants and encouraging them to use the language regularly.

I also see this frequently in friends from certain cities, specifically New York. Yes, it's one of the world's major centers for business, culture, and people. Being the biggest does not automatically carry a parallel "being the best."

However, living in a fishbowl of any size can woo us into a false sense that we are in the center of things. Everyone revolves around us. False. We remain culturally ignorant in the scope of the world.

That said, I cannot get interested in being politically correct. Nor do I feel a need to be correct... at any price. I do not mind when people disagree with me. I do not mind someone else being politically correct as long as they do not mind me being politically incorrect.

I do not let someone else's outrage over my opinions sully my passion.

I think we get too wrapped up in what other people will think. They have the right to their opinions, just as we all do.

Bimbo Basics

To me, truth often seems unreal or surreal... especially when it's not our conception of what the truth *should* be. While it's easier to hang out with like-minded people, that also makes us more close-minded. How boring it would be if we all thought the same way about everything?!?!

We have been disagreeing with each other since humans came into existence. I don't expect it to stop anytime soon.

When people take our points of disagreement to the level of outrage, I get dismayed. The labeling and name-calling and hatred spewed is saddening, if not maddening. We humans have definitely not evolved as much as we'd like to think.

Look at our humor. We hear the same thing. One person says, "That's funny!" The person next to them says, "That's *not* funny!"

A bipartisan sense of humor helps. Of course, bi-partisan humorists help even more. I think we've all heard lines that poke fun at both sides of the aisle. Case in point: If con is the opposite of pro, then is Congress the opposite of progress?

We all need to choose not to drink "the whine of losers." I like it when politicians from both sides of the aisle have a great sense of humor, especially when they can laugh at themselves.

The Bimbo Has *MORE* Brains

"Being President is like running a cemetery. You've got a lot of people under you, and nobody's listening."
-- William J. Clinton (1946 -)
42nd President of the United States

Most of us don't have original thoughts. I don't expect to start now or any time soon. Even when we think or say something that seems clever, it was likely thought or said by someone in some configuration at some time in the near or distant past. Here's one good example.

"Everyone is entitled to their own opinion, but not their own facts."
-- Daniel Patrick Moynihan (1927 – 2003)
American Politician and Sociologist; US Senator from New York

The previous quote appears in a March, 2003, Daniel Patrick Moynihan memorandum. In 2016, this became attributed to Democratic Presidential Nominee Hillary Clinton, who used it when trying to slam Donald Trump.

Let's shift away from politics and look at a more personal aspect of political correctness. These are just a few quick thoughts on how we relate with other people.

For example, for far too long, personal relationships were defined by standards that turned out to be double standards. Another of my husband's "Ronnerisms" emerged when I pointed out that he was applying a double standard. With all innocence and sincerity, Ron retorted, "I am *not* using a double standard. I am simply saying that there is one set of rules for you and another set for me." I burst out laughing.

That is no laughing matter in some cultures. In the U.S.A., we are blessed with the opportunities to make better and fairer choices.

With regard to that, I consider our most precious personal relationships as Basics. For example, if you choose to marry, try to marry someone you can enjoy and trust as your best friend for the rest of your life.

Bimbo Basics

Be with someone worthy of you. Someone who respects you. Someone who works hard, is not a pushover, and who is smart. A great sense of humor helps you survive almost anything... that's yours and his sense of humor.

These choices are difficult. Often we find ourselves in a relationship and getting married as the next obvious step. We need to try to look back at how the relationship got started. Unfortunately, if he's a handsome, confidant "lady's man," we can be pretty sure that won't change if we marry him.

We forget that he really wasn't just flirting with us. However, we *want* to believe that we're something special to *some*body. This type of man makes us feel that way. Unfortunately, they are good at making *lots* of women feel special. Run away.

In both our personal and business relationships, observe how someone treats other people. Are they kind or demeaning? Supportive or controlling? Understanding or demanding? Observe their behavior, tone, words, and attitudes toward cab drivers, wait staff, telemarketers, etc. This will quickly teach you a great deal about this person's character.

Take care to not play games with people. Those who do are pushing for control. They tend to get a lot of satisfaction out of keeping others off balance. It's bogus, but it's a clear reflection of their insecurities.

Social tattoos are rather dopey. Never tattoo someone's name on your body. These are not just piercings you can let grow in when you change your mind. You can't change tattooed body art as easily as you can change clothes or jewelry. I recall Jimmy Buffett defining a tattoo rather well when he called it a permanent reminder of a temporary feeling.

Tip: Laugh at yourself. We need to remember not to take ourselves too seriously. Nobody else does.

15
Spontaneous Exhaustion

Just as spontaneous combustion gives us instant flames where there didn't seem to even be heat, spontaneous exhaustion happens when we are done thinking for the time and just want to fall asleep.

Of course, we have had spontaneous adjusion. This happens when someone is immediately presumed guilty of something though they've yet said or done nothing. My husband, Ron, does this with me. I won't have done anything, but he delivers one of his famed Ronnerisms. He'll wryly admit, "I'm not saying you're responsible. I'm just saying that I'm blaming you for it." There it is. Spontaneous adjusion.

Spontaneity is fascinating. I know I am frequently entertaining friends with little or no notice. Friends marvel that I come up with a lovely meal or array of appetizers and tapas at the drop of a hat, so to speak. Ah, but I believe that excelling at spontaneity does not happen automatically.

To be good at spontaneity takes careful planning.

On the other hand, spontaneous exhaustion takes no planning. It simply happens. You know those moments when you have heard enough. The ranting just needs to stop. We get sick and tired of being sick and tired.

Sometimes I think there are people out there who spend their days thinking about the next theme or topic to unravel. What can I do to disrupt the status quo... to muss up someone's plan... to rain on their parade.

Other times I think they mean no harm, but we humans can get all "wrapped up in our shorts" so to speak. In 2017 we heard lots of ranting about the need to tear down all the statues in our nation that depict leaders of the Confederacy. Removing statues does not change our history.

Our history, just as any nation's history, has not always been pretty. It reflects our struggles. These statues reflect our struggles and history, too.

Remember Charlottesville, Virginia? The City Council voted to remove a statue of General Robert E. Lee, Commander of the Confederate army. One month later, groups filed suit, protesting the statue's removal since it violated a state law protecting war memorials and also violated the deed through which the monument had been donated to the city.

Two months after that a group of nationalists scheduled an event in the park to protest the statue's removal. Despite it being a scheduled event, the mayor and other politicians were angry, saying the statue intimidated minorities. A social media explosion of words and hatred from both sides resulted.

Three months later, as the permitted event approached, it became increasingly clear that clash was inevitable. Counter-protesters planned a rally to thwart the nationalists. Violence was planned. Both sides got prepared.

Violence erupted, as it will when extremists clash. One person was killed.

The hatred spewed from both sides was abhorrent. The violence was tragic. The political drivel appalled me and inspired spontaneous exhaustion.

Civic "leaders" had let this pot simmer for months, all because the mayor insisted on removing the Confederate General's statue and changing the name Robert E. Lee Park to Emancipation Park.

Now, I hail from north of that Mason-Dixon line, so my ancestors fought on the union side in the war that divided this country. That said, 620,000 American soldiers died in the Civil War. 620,000. It matters not for which side they were fighting. They were Americans.

The war was not just fought over the issue of slavery. Trying to now get all politically correct and eliminate evidence or monuments of the Confederacy is ludicrous.

Traveling to and walking through Civil War battlefield historic sites, such as Gettysburg, is extraordinarily moving for any American. We can literally feel our history.

There are many other historic places that commemorate Civil War battles. I remember visiting one in Chattanooga, Tennessee that completely broke my heart. If you are ever in the Chattanooga area, definitely check out the National Military Park. Lookout Mountain is amazing! I was stunned by the hundreds of monuments... everywhere. They recognize soldiers from all over our nation... North and South. The 1863 battles here were painful and decisive.

Now with all this PC thinking, I learned that people were wondering when or if officials would remove the monuments that represent the Confederacy.

People! Such thinking is spontaneously exhausting!

There are some 14-hundred monuments in this one park. Yes. One thousand, four hundred monuments. The national rant to remove such monuments has gotten way out of control.

Thankfully, officials at the Park are not following the lead of the Mayor of Charlottesville, Virginia. Instead, they are observing that these monuments are and should be protected as the historic properties that they are.

It's history. It's powerful. We should not try to diminish it.

It seems that we cannot help ourselves. In 2017, I also started hearing rumblings by the "PC Police" that we needed to get rid of Columbus Day. Well, okay. Christopher Columbus was a hot-shot explorer of his day. Despite what we were likely taught in school, however, he did not discover America. After all, the Vikings had settlements in North America long before Columbus sailed the ocean blue. Centuries before their boats landed, the very first human immigrants had walked across what we call the Bering Strait on what was then a narrow strip of land from Asia to North America. They continued to migrate and populate North and South America.

Plus, Columbus was involved in the extraordinarily popular, world-wide trade of the time... slavery. Insidious human trafficking. So, we assuredly don't want to celebrate that. However, it is part of our young nation's history. Ignoring or turning our backs on history does not change it. What is spontaneously exhausting is failing to learn from our history. That is a big part of what destines nations to repeat it. We assuredly don't want *that*.

That said, in the time of Christopher Columbus, the "known world" (primarily that which was known by Europeans) was very actively participating in slavery and had been for a great many generations. Yes, that includes all the African nations. Africans enslaved each other. Africans sold each other into slavery. Even those we have referred to as Indians or native Americans enslaved members of other tribes.

Columbus Day opponents express a preference to celebrate Native American Day instead. Hmmm... As with most labels we give groups of people, trends change.

But wait, if we turn Columbus Day into Native American Day or Indigenous People Day, we are actually celebrating people who also enslaved other people. See, spontaneous exhaustion. It's all so very tiring.

We humans have long suffered Man's inhumanity to Man.

No matter what we try, we aren't apt to get politically correct or out of trouble on this one. What we should note is the fact that slavery is far more than an issue of whites enslaving blacks. On our U.S. soil, however, whites enslaving blacks became the most grotesque and large-scale enslavement of people in recent history.

In truth, when babies were born to slaves, weren't those babies actually native to America and not Africa? Who is a native American anyway? Years ago it became unpopular to use the word Indians when referring to the people living here when the bulk of European explorers and settlers started arriving. After all, Columbus had failed to reach his destination... India. So, the name was a misnomer that stuck... for centuries.

Now, for example, if I say that I was born in New York, people would call me a native New Yorker. So, if I am born in America, I am a native American. I did not move here from somewhere else. I am a native, regardless of how many centuries or moments my parents may have been here first. As I've said, I just don't capitalize the "n" in native.

When someone asks our ethnic heritage, whether or not we've had DNA testing done, we readily reply with what we know. We might say something like, "I am Irish." Or, "I am Italian-American." Or, "I am African-American." Or, "I am a mixture of Greek, French, and British Isles." Or whatever.

We are Americans. We are frequently what I call a "Heinz 57" blend. Each and every one of us is a perfect recipe, a mixture of our familial history. Delicious!

That is just fine. I am proud to be an American. I don't need to refer to myself by my heritage or ethnic background. I don't say, "I'm Eurasian." That is my ethnic background, but my particular blend only comes up when someone specifically asks my background. Then I can say that I am a blend of Armenian, English, Irish, Scottish, Welsh, Dutch, Italian, and the big surprise... 15% Scandinavian. Oh, those Vikings.

Spontaneous Exhaustion

The bottom line is that I was born here, so I am an American. I wasn't a naturalized citizen, so I am a native American. I do not say, "I'm a Eurasian-American." I say, "I'm an American." Most of us do, I think. We are not slighting our heritage. We are merely recognizing our place of birth or home or both.

All this aside, I "get" the thinking that calling a holiday by a person's name could be failing to recognize other people of the same stature, thinking, or fame. Thus, for example, we no longer celebrate the birthdays of Presidents Abraham Lincoln and George Washington. We did when I was younger. We celebrated Lincoln's Birthday *and* Washington's Birthday.

Then someone had the idea of making major holidays fall on Mondays to provide consistency and long weekends. So, since those two birthdays were close together anyway, they were merged into one national holiday we call Presidents Day.

Oooh, I'm tired again. It's this spontaneous exhaustion.

With that thinking, those who advocated calling Martin Luther King, Jr.'s birthday "Civil Rights Day" may well have been on the right track. Whew! *That* may annoy you, unless consistency is important to you.

Tip: Perhaps we'd all benefit if we stopped trying to be so politically correct that we become downright quacky.

16
Media and Other Mayhem

"Work isn't work unless you'd rather be doing something else."
                                        -- Don Shula (1930 -)
                                        NFL Coach)

Working as a journalist, I heard quips like, "If you annoyed both sides on a story, you probably got it right." It's never easy to keep our personal feelings and sensibilities out of a story, but it's a journalist's job to constantly try. Sometimes we fear that we may lean too far in a direction that is opposite from how we feel, simply because we are overcompensating for our own opinions.

One year following the conviction of a young woman in a heinous and highly-publicized murder trial following the death of her husband, I was interviewing the murderess' mother. She very sincerely expressed herself when she told me that she could always tell exactly how journalists, both national and local, felt about her daughter... which ones believed that Pamela Smart had been guilty or innocent. Except for me. I had been the news anchor and had introduced many a related story and interview, but her mother said she had not been able to tell where I stood. During this half-hour interview show, she truly thought that I would finally reveal myself to her. I didn't. I merely said, "Then I was doing my job."

At this point I was no longer anchoring the news. I was hosting a live studio audience talk show. I was able to share my opinions openly. In comparison with being a news journalist, this is what we call a commentator. As a talk show host or commentator we can comment on topics. This is something we must not do as a journalist. Our quips and slants on any topic are off limits and must not be shared with our audience.

We see a lot of newscasters walk a very fine line in this regard when they serve as moderators at political debates. We all know that moderators should ask questions to draw information from candidates to help voters understand each candidate's positions on important issues, right? Instead, far too often, we find moderators salivating to get their "gotcha" questions asked to try to make particular candidates stumble. Worse yet, we see "journalists" tossing what we call softball questions to candidates they personally support. Seriously. This is not journalism.

It makes me see how people get frustrated with what they call "fake news." People present themselves as journalists but then show their slant, their opinion, a one-sided look at what's going on. I don't care if you believe it's CNN, Fox News, ABC, or any other mainstream media outlet that's being one-sided. You can rightfully believe someone is delivering fake news if they are presenting a one-sided slant. Like it or not, they have taken a news item and turned it into opinion.

We start to get into what I call Opinion Bleeders and Leaders. Bleeders simply rant because they hold popular opinions, and their fans will cheer them for voicing parallel beliefs. Leaders are working with facts and maintaining their credibility.

It's tough. When we work in news, we tend to become close to the stories. People understand that we have more information on a particular topic, so they often ask for our opinions. We can only share them when not working.

Conservative political commentator Tucker Carlson talked with retiring television journalist and commentator Britt Hume, prior to starting his new program on November 14, 2016 on Fox. Carlson said that the media was losing credibility fast with viewers due to faux pas such as Donna Brazile (Democrat party strategist; interim chairperson for Democratic National Committee) leaking so-called "town hall questions" to Hillary Clinton before the debate.

Whether we like what Carlson said or not is not relevant. As a commentator, he is permitted and even encouraged to offer opinions and stir debate.

On the other hand, journalists are supposed to keep their opinions to themselves. It's not easy. We are human.

The Bimbo Has *MORE* Brains

On June 6, 2017, I watched CNN news anchor Ana Cabrera toss a story to a White House correspondent, noting President Trump's response to a reporter who'd asked if he had any words for James Comey as he went in to testify. President Trump had said, "I wish him luck." No problem. That was all fact.

My eyebrows were raised as I then heard the CNN anchor and reporter scoff. Jim Acosta, the White House correspondent added, "And if you believe that, I have a bridge to sell you."

Yes, he said this. Hmmm… not even close to journalism. I call this opinion, plus "attitude." There are no more words he could speak that would hold credibility.

Meanwhile, I must note that when individuals from any news source cross the line of journalism, I do not take it as a reflection on their peers. I believe that most reporters work very hard to report the facts… just the facts.

CNN Anchor, Jake Trapper, reported in early June of 2017 that investigators said there was no evidence, not even circumstantial evidence, that shows anything illegal done by Donald Trump or his campaigners. Investigators had found no collusion evidence, and yet, proponents were still desperately wanting them to seek anything that could suggest some sort of negative issue with Trump or his supporters.

We seem stuck in this mode where we feel determined to make our wishful thinking become real. We keep stating the same things over and over, as if that will somehow validate our opinion.

In some horrific situations, personal vents reveal some dark hearts. CBS fired a top legal executive for making "deeply inappropriate comments." After the Las Vegas Country Music Festival shooting massacre where a gunman fired wildly into a crowd of some 22,000, she'd posted on Facebook that she was "not even sympathetic" to the hundreds of shooting victims. Her rationale was that "country music fans often are Republican gun toters."

You may also recall a major network anchor getting into hot water when a gunman fired into a Congressional Republican softball game practice, seriously wounding Representative Steve Scalise. This anchorman had expressed that the wounds received by Republicans were "self-inflicted," as if it was *their* fault.

This is how hoaxes displace facts. This is how we inflate theories, opinions, slants, and slivers of truth. This is how fake news is born.

Is it just satire or humor? I do not believe so, not when we paint it as "news." Regardless, we've all heard about fake news so much that it's beyond tiresome.

However, I do note a lot of attention being paid to what I call a "faux reality." We achieve this by applying a simple technique called Distract & Divide.

Look at the way syndicated columnist Michelle Malkin writes and speaks. She casually notes the "left-wing zealots'" panic over "Islamophobia" as have been spawned by "multiple acts of Islamo-faux-bia." That's right. "Faux" as in f-a-u-x. She has documented numerous acts by Muslims to stir up unfounded fear and public attention, creating a false reality.

These deliberate "distract and divide" ploys generate media coverage and get people spewing about white supremacists and other groups perceived as hating Muslims. When these incidents turn out to have been committed by Muslims, the media has typically downplayed or ignored it completely.

Bad news sells. Delusion sells.

That's why commentary programs are so popular on television. Panel members or guests talk over each other… constantly. Perhaps I should say, yell over each other.

In the 1960's, we had lots of protests and sit-ins. They were mostly anti-war and pro-civil rights. There were other themes too, ranging from lowering the voting and drinking ages to eliminating school dress codes and legalizing drugs. Meanwhile, we had lots of "Flower Children," dancing and chanting, marching and protesting, calling for love, not war.

There were also a few groups who would travel hundreds of miles to join protests. In those days they did it because they believed in the "cause" of the particular protest. In this day, we seem plagued by huge groups of paid protestors and counter protestors. Both sides try to scream down the other side. No one appears to be interested in listening to anyone else. Too often it's hard to see the original protestors.

I enjoy watching media coverage and even analysis of these events. It lets me see that there are still a lot of good reporters out there. I have a great many friends who have worked or are still working in the news industry. I feel very blessed to be able to say that with very rare exceptions, they are some of "the good guys." They are honest, compassionate, intelligent, fair-minded journalists. This cannot be easy when living in today's splintering media markets and under intense social media microscopes.

As a newscaster, I think that we had it easier back in the 1980's and 90's. With dramatically fewer channels to choose and no ocean of social media washing over us, we became like family to our audiences. We were in their kitchens and living rooms and family rooms every single day or night.

We worked hard to earn our audience's respect by taking what we did seriously, but not taking ourselves too seriously. Respect. Integrity. No sensationalism. These were key thoughts in our daily work. We wanted to be good role models, not celebrity idols.

I learned a great deal from the wonderful journalists with whom I worked. I especially appreciate today how thoughtful, fair, and down-to-earth they were. They were not glory hounds. They were passionate, yet objective. They were smart, yet sassy. They worked hard, yet held great senses of humor. They loved people and loved working.

Media and Other Mayhem

While working in television, we can lose sight of the influence we have on people. We expect to drift into distant memory within weeks of leaving the field. It can be both shocking and very humbling to learn that people remember for not just weeks, but for decades.

More than twenty years after leaving local television, folks continue to strike up conversations with me wherever we happen to meet. I've been at the deli counter or grocery store check-out line and had people grab my arm, as they suddenly gush about recognizing my laughter or voice. Or they start up a conversation with me in the aisles while shopping. They share everything from how much they admired me to having wanted to grow up to "be" me. It's extremely overwhelming and humbling, even today. Perhaps even more today.

We have had so many changes in influence. We have so many more outlets washing us with information and hype. It can all seem overwhelming. Yet, I still think keeping a good sense of humor is vital.

"You know the world is off tilt when the best rapper is a white guy, the best golfer is a black guy, the tallest basketball player is Chinese, and the Germans don't want to go to war."
-- Charles Barkley (1963 -)
American Basketball Player
&
-- Chris Rock (1965 -)
American Comedian

I have heard that previous quote attributed to both Rock and Barkley. I am unsure which man may have said it first nor who may have paraphrased the other. Their humor is clear.

When looking at media, I don't want to ignore non-news programing. I guess I blame the enormous volume of programming out there now for the tired, bland, and inconsistent quality of shows. Programs that hold a strong team of writers seem few and far between.

That has caused me to grow tired of much of what's out there. Even the promotions that are supposed to entice me stir absolutely no interest in me.

I have even less interest in so-called reality shows featuring wanna-be celebrities clawing their way through one dysfunctional scenario to another... or some new collection of beautiful people getting all emotional as they try to date and get to know each other under the constant scrutiny of cameras, all in hopes of finding their soul mate. Nor do I care to watch the latest variation on co-naked survival in the everglades or on some remote island.

Life is just too short and too precious to spend even minutes watching drivel on television.

I blame it on the splintered market. More clearly, TV times have changed. Instead of three, four, or even five major networks, there are dozens upon dozens. With hundreds of channels serving up programming, no wonder what I call lack-of-reality shows abound. Finding enough good writers, directors, actors, crew, and such to have quality programming with great storylines for every time slot on every network would be daunting.

Call me old-fashioned, but I enjoy a well-written, well-produced, and well-performed show, with great characters and even some socially-redeeming value tucked in for good measure. Favorite programs tend to be clever "dramadies" like "Castle" (2009-2016) and "NCIS" (since 2003) and the ol' stand-by dramas like "Law and Order" (1990-2010) and "Law and Order: SVU" (Since 1999).

Sir Ronald, my husband, is more into shows with plenty of action, sex, or violence, so he tends toward the likes of "Game of Thrones" (since 2011) and "The Transporter." Other well-written dramas of note include "Mad Men" (2007-2015), "The Sopranos" (1999-2007), "24" (2001-10), and "ER" (1994-2009).

Perhaps I am jaded when it comes to comedies, but I am rarely a fan of today's assortment of television comedies. For me, today's comedies seem more about cheap humor, void of the punch of social relevance, snappy one-liners, sassy characters, and great delivery that earmarked great comedies of the past. I am sad about this, because I love to laugh.

I loved the programs of my childhood… "I Love Lucy" (1951-57) and "The Dick Van Dyke Show" (1961 – 66). Then came more classics, including "The Carol Burnett Show" (1967-78), "The Mary Tyler Moore Show" (1970-77), "All in the Family" (1971-79), and "Mash" (1972 – 83). The 1980's introduced more great comedy classics, including "Cheers" (1982 – 93), "The Cosby Show" (1984-92), and "Seinfeld" (1989 – 98). Since then, worthy comedy series have, in my opinion waned, with a few exceptions, including "Frasier" (1993-2004), "Friends" (1994-2004), and "30 Rock" (2006-13).

I am glad that many networks choose to share the old stand-by classics from various decades, plus we can choose to download many whenever we want. Regardless of your personal favorite comedies of the past, it's easy to see that they just don't write them like that anymore.

Of course, public scrutiny may be to blame here. Remember, we are overly focused on being politically correct. While we have shows like "Black-ish" (since 2014) and "The Good Place" (since 2016), I find most comedic writing to be trying and failing to hit social hot buttons without resorting to low comedy, such as the mockumentary-styled "Modern Family" (since 2009). It's just sadly difficult for writers to deliver actuality without alerting the PC Police.

Tip:

"Nothing great was ever achieved without enthusiasm."
-- Ralph Waldo Emerson (1803 – 1882)
American Essayist and Poet

17
New American Revolution

"The truth will set you free. But first, it will piss you off."
-- Gloria Steinem
American Political Activist
(1934 -)

Many voted for Hillary Clinton BECAUSE she was a Democrat.
Many voted for Donald Trump DESPITE his being a Republican.

Republican leadership did so much in-fighting throughout the
Primary season, they lost their perspective on the people. They
needed to go into the back room, so to speak, fight it out among
themselves, and narrow it down. Leave the "blood on the walls,"
but come out of that back room singing the same song.

Think about it. GOP leadership didn't like the candidate the people
in their party chose to see as President. Consider this: Perhaps it's
time to evolve the primary season rules to ensure that by January
first, for example, the field is narrowed down to 3 candidates. Then
there is a far greater likelihood of having primary election and
caucus results that stir a true majority of support for someone,
regardless of the opinions held by party leaders.

2015 into 2016 showed Republican ridiculousness with a field of 82
candidates. Okay, I exaggerate, but it makes the point that it's
unseemly, at best, to complain about the results of your own
process simply because it didn't play out in favor of someone's
favored candidate. Just as too many cooks spoil the soup, too many
egos spoil the candidate field.

Naysayers were confident that the non-politician, Donald Trump,
would implode somewhere along the line. Instead, his support
grew to include Republicans, Independents, and Democrats.

When Republican naysayers chose what I saw as an arrogant path,
pooh-poohing the candidacy of Donald Trump, I knew it was the

end of the Republican Party as they had known it. The New American Revolution was afoot!

> *"If particular care and attention is not paid to the ladies, we are determined to foment a rebellion, and will not hold ourselves bound by any laws in which we have no voice or representation."*
> --Abigail Adams (1744 - 1818)
> First Lady to the 2nd President of the United States

240 years after the first American Revolution, we entered another one. This one was a philosophical and political revolution. Just as the one in 1776, this one started quietly and grew. This one started within the Republican Party.

As I noted in my 2016 **The Bimbo Has Brains** book, this marked the first time in many, many decades that the American people stood up en masse and rejected the political machine of either party.

Our differences make us stronger. If any one party maintains leadership for too long, however, it's time for the checks and balances to kick in, or our nation gets warped in one way or another. We were at that point during the Obama administration.

Change had been promised. However, the changes we got were not what many would consider to be positive changes. Divisiveness, hatred, racism, and violence escalated to all-time highs. Our nation was in deep trouble.

Still, just because change is desperately needed, we do not know if positive changes can emerge out of the muck and mire of the politically entangled mess in Washington.

Then the 2016 Presidential Primary process began. Herds of candidates shifted from polite respect of each other to throwing increasingly sharp barbs at opponents. Whether we knew it or not, the first shots had been fired in the New American Revolution.

I did not know if the people could or truly would be able to rise up and win this Revolution.

The Bimbo Has *MORE* Brains

There he was, "The Donald," with no political experience. Critics laughed. Media scoffed. Republicans said he'd implode, get bored, and be gone. Democrats sniffed that it would be great if he won, since they could so easily beat him.

The voters were not laughing. The people increasingly recognized his lack of political savvy, but were drawn his sincerity on the issues that matter to this nation. He captured the hearts and minds of millions of people, many of whom had never before felt inspired to vote... Many of whom, for the first time, felt this NON-political candidate held out the hope they desperately sought.

Then, we also had the fact that the general election ballot would feature the first woman in U.S. history to have received the nomination from one of the two major parties. She was the "stand by your man" First Lady. She'd become a U.S. Senator. She'd served as U.S. Secretary of State. Surely, Hillary Clinton was the most experienced and qualified candidate on either ballot.

Regardless, voters in both parties shrieked at the very mention of the top candidates' names. I mean, who on earth in their right mind would want a Presidential candidate, never mind a President, who is arrogant, divisive, egotistical, or a hateful bigot?

That question asked, if you were a fan of Hillary Clinton, you naturally know that I was just describing Donald Trump. Then again, if you were a fan of Donald Trump, you naturally know that I was just describing Hillary Clinton.

Quite frankly, I'm tired of politicians pointing at each other and squawking about an opponent being the very same negative things they themselves may be presenting.

By the general election, millions of voters dared fly in the face of both major political parties. Many registered Democrats, although few openly admitted it prior to the election, actually crossed over and voted for Donald Trump. Most independent voters chose Trump.

Whether voters like him or not, Donald Trump stood up to the system, noted politicos, Washington, media, academia, and his own Hollywood buddies.

Whether voters like her or not, had Hillary Clinton won the election, many feared that the divisiveness that had pervaded the nation for nearly a decade would have grown stronger.

Following the election, many Americans felt fearful. They had believed that Hillary Clinton would prevail, and the status quo would be maintained.

Instead, the boat was rocking. The groundswell of Donald Trump's New American Revolution grew stronger, as more people than ever before felt empowered.

Despite the claims by pundits and Democrat leaders, a great many women would absolutely not consider voting for Hillary Clinton. While most people think it would be wonderful to see a woman become President of the United States, she was definitely not seen as the *right* woman by millions of women.

I respect that. We shouldn't vote for a woman just because we want to see a woman become President. That would be like voting for somebody who is Black or Hispanic or Asian simply because we want to see a Black or Hispanic or Asian person become President.

Politicians and political insiders should never allow themselves to think "they" know more about what the people want and need than the people. Regardless of party, that thinking laid the groundwork for an ideological, philosophical, political, and demographic revolution.

Battles raged through pollsters throughout the long months of the primary and straight through the General Election. The media bombarded the public with constant flurries of negative political malarkey. Candidates themselves increasingly appeared to be their own worst enemies.

The Bimbo Has *MORE* Brains

"New opinions often appear first as jokes and fancies,
then as blasphemies and treason, then as questions open to discussion,
and finally as established truths."

-- George Bernard Shaw
Irish Playwright & Political Activist
(1856 – 1950)

With as little as three weeks to go until the Presidential election, polls showed Hillary Clinton as much as 9 and 10 points ahead of Donald Trump. Although, as my husband pointed out, the Democrats must have felt some sort of "pinch," as Clinton pulled out the stops with lots of last-minute campaigning in states like Pennsylvania and Michigan, which most had believed were shoo-ins for her. Donald Trump won both states, despite Hollywood's best efforts to shore up Clinton's predicted landslide victory with their fan bases.

Perhaps we should have seen it coming. If we listened to the mass media, we thought Clinton would win. However, my husband and I had seen what should have told us that middle America was not interested in Hillary Clinton for President. Just days before the general election, Ron and I drove through the states of Pennsylvania, Virginia, West Virginia, North Carolina, South Carolina, Georgia, and Florida. We saw lots of signs hailing Donald Trump for President... Make America Great Again. We did not see one single sign advocating Hillary Clinton, unless you count the "Clinton for Prison" signs.

Voters were quietly determined to take back America.

This political race had pointed out something we had not previously seen so clearly. We were a divided nation. We had become the elite versus middle America.

In truth, when the dust settled, small town America, quiet Republicans, and most independent voters came out to fight the fight in the ballot box. The New American Revolution, started during the Primary season, was poised for the ultimate Election Day showdown.

Politicos confidently patted themselves on the backs and prepared for Clinton's victory party. Media types coyly asked Donald Trump subtle questions about what his plans might be following the election... in the chance that he did not win, of course.

Poof!

Donald Trump, a non-politician, took the country by storm. If not for the "citified" New York and California effect, the 2016 election would have marked the biggest landslide victory since Ronald Reagan in 1984. While Donald Trump lost the overall popular vote, he won more states. He won more counties, Trump landing 2,622 counties to Clinton's 490, though hers included those with much larger population densities. He won more than any other Republican since Ronald Reagan.

Some called it a shocker... a surprise... an upset victory. However, what we failed to see and what the media failed to cover is one basic fact. To opponents of Hillary Clinton, the election results were seen as a great relief... answered prayers... a hard-fought victory.

In hindsight, I was reminded somewhat of George H.W. Bush's bid for a second term. His ratings were so outstandingly high, that the Republican leadership seemed to skip campaigning. They prepared for the victory party.

Bush lost. This time it had happened to the Democrats.

More interesting to me were some reality slices that flared in the election aftermath. While Clinton supporters had reveled in labeling Trump as divisive, of weak temperament, and a hate-monger, Clinton supporters also revealed the actual divisiveness and hatred in this nation, venting election loss disappointment with violence, smashing people's car windshields and ransacking shops.

The Bimbo Has *MORE* Brains

I respect the 2016 Presidential election protestors who peacefully expressed concern for the tone in America following the election of Donald Trump. Few could have predicted, however, that fellow Democrats would embody the most dangerous things they had ever feared in Trump.

I must step back on one item. Some had also labeled Donald Trump a misogynist. From my perspective, these people have likely never known a misogynist. Trump does not come across at all like one. Neither women who have been married to him nor those who have worked for him have ever used such a label.

However, they could have *rightly* claimed that in Trump's not-so-distant past he'd said and done things that could earn him a label such as "sexist." But that hardly is cause for a nation to fear him as a leader.

Bill Clinton was adored while he was President, and he'd behaved as a sexist for most of his life, including his time in the Oval Office. Further, out of the millions and millions of men in this nation, the percentage is extremely minute that have never spoken as nor behaved as sexists on more than one occasion.

Ah, but we should remember. We don't want to let the facts get in the way of a good story.

There <u>are</u> things that Donald Trump said… often repeatedly… that are legitimate reasons for concern. This is the case with *all* candidates, including Hillary Clinton.

Would he really build a wall along the Mexican border? Such a wall would *not* be meant to prevent travel, immigration, or legal workers. Such a wall *would* be meant to prevent the flood of *illegal* immigration by people anxious to hold out their hands for freebies, paid for by American citizens.

The wall was an issue that sharply divided voters. Most likely, the controversy arose out of fear and misinformation, far more than facts.

New American Revolution

Certainly, not all protesters were disappointed Hillary supporters. I believe her disappointed supporters exercised their right to peaceful protest. This was fine. This was respected, in fact.

By the 3rd day of protests over the election of Donald Trump, it came out that radical left-wing groups were leading and spreading violence. International groups, including anti-Semitics, also were on hand encouraging and leading destruction.

This may be how they protest abroad, but they have now brought it here. Worse than even their ignorance of our peaceful election process is the manner in which people were teaching *our* young citizens to follow their lead.

I heard people call the outbreaks "temper tantrums." I saw it as worse. I saw good, worthy, and respected peaceful protests getting sullied by violence. This was *not* violence to protest a fair election, won by the opposing Party. This was violence against fellow Americans and their property. There was no excuse.

Regardless of the candidate for whom we cast our vote in the 2016 U.S. Presidential election, it seems to horrify some people that Donald Trump got a far wider field of support than they expected. His voters proved to be people of all ages, all races, all religions, and widely varied cultural backgrounds. Both men and women. Gay and straight. Natural born citizens and legal immigrants. Republicans, Democrats, and independent voters.

The same can be said of the voters who chose Hillary Clinton.

While both candidates reviled most voters at some point, Americans had made a decision. Some may have simply selected the candidate they hated less… or the candidate they believed would most likely bring the change they believed the nation needed.

Let me repeat. We, as a nation, definitely wanted change. Immediately following the election, on Wednesday morning, November 9th, 2016, House speaker Paul Ryan explained the election results this way. He said, "Seven of ten Americans did not like the direction this country was going."

Still, people nationwide were in shock at the results. My mother said that Donald Trump had won because "ordinary people that live in small towns all over this country made the effort to go out and vote."

Big cities like Los Angeles and New York City were not happy to be undone by middle America. We had known it *could* happen, but we didn't quite believe it *would* happen.

Turn the tables for a moment. In 2008 and again in 2012, when Barack Obama was elected and then re-elected President, an enormous number of Americans was disappointed... terrified at the prospect of our Nation's future. They expressed the *exact* same sentiments that we heard from young and inner-city Democrats following the election of Donald Trump in 2016.

However, they did not take to the streets, start shoving matches with police, smash automobile windows, or ransack shops. They did not cover their faces or participate in violent protests. They didn't attack people they knew or believed had voted for Obama. They didn't block traffic or wield baseball bats and clubs against their fellow Americans or their property.

Their hearts were broken. Their fears were enlivened. Their prayers had gone unanswered. They knew they needed to do a better job next time at the ballot box.

Where was President Barack Obama to speak to the nation about respecting each other and our election process? I remember how quick he was to publicly rail against a police officer who had overreacted in shooting a youthful offender. Now we had lots of offenders, lots of violence, and lots of silence from the President.

Where was Nancy Pelosi, the Democrats' leader in the Senate? All leaders should have been immediately calling for calm, rational, peaceful behavior.

Why did violent protestors believe for a nanosecond that anyone would ever believe their open displays of violence, racism, bigotry, and hatred were legitimate responses to the election of a man they feared due to a belief that he wanted and supported violence, racism, bigotry, and hatred? Talk about hypocrites! They redefined the word in a most grotesque fashion.

Cowardly violence lessens the impact of legitimate and peaceful protests.

Ironically, it was the so-called hate-mongers, divisive racists, and bigots who voted for Donald Trump who took the high road, wielding the ballot box. Who wielded baseball bats instead?

Extraordinarily hateful true colors of disrespect, violence, and destructive thinking blossomed into hideous actions. We'd seen hints of this as nay-sayers harassed and intimidated Trump supporters trying to access Trump rallies. We saw pockets of full-blown, anti-American, domestic terrorism after he won the election.

I have always observed that a powerful difference in this nation is that we can argue vehemently with each other over politics, but once a decision is made, we let it go and work with each other, rather than bashing our opponents' supporters or harming property.

It is *not* the American way to physically attack folks because of differing ideologies. *That* is bigotry and fascism. We look at it as going against our rights as Americans at the very least, and often it is downright criminal. It's outrageous. It makes dissenters look ignorant and out of touch. It also reveals that they lack the "core values" they alleged to support. However, I must believe that the majority of Hillary Clinton supporters had to have been totally mortified at the violent protestors' actions.

Even a year after he took office, it remains interesting that the very people still pointing fingers at Donald Trump, accusing him of hatred, bigotry, anger-mongering, and divisive insecurity, are the same exact people who were and are spewing dramatically *more* hate-speak, bigotry-inspiring divisiveness, and anger than Donald Trump had in his most robust outbursts.

Further, the anti-Trump violence, masked as protests of his victory, reflect animosity toward fellow Americans, rather than toward him. Hate-filled, disrespectful mindsets are now firmly entrenched in the U.S.A., and they turned out to *not* be in the NRA-leaning GOP. It all came from the so-called, self-dubbed "Progressives," who have now proven themselves to be "Regressives."

Whether voters were voting *for* Donald Trump or *against* Hillary Clinton is of little matter. That was the General Election. Americans by the millions voted for Donald Trump and toppled what he'd repeatedly noted as a "rigged system."

> *"In a time of universal deceit,*
> *telling the truth becomes a revolutionary act."*
> -- George Orwell
> English Novelist & Journalist
> (1903 – 1950)

My Aunt is a big fan of Rush Limbaugh. She particularly enjoyed his November, 2016 newsletter, in which he had gotten the General Election "right" three weeks ahead of the election. While he admitted that no one really knew what the actual results would be, he painted a very clear picture of the "monster vote" that could give Trump a strong victory. Limbaugh referred to the "monster vote" as the same, unaccounted for and unpredicted vote of the people that gave Ronald Reagan a double-digit victory <u>and</u> stunned Britain during the Brexit referendum to opt out of the European Union. Rush Limbaugh said that no matter what happened on November 8, 2016, "We won't quit. There is no defeat here."

Had Hillary Clinton pulled off a victory, I somehow doubt that Trump voters would have taken to the streets to smash up cars and businesses. I do believe they would have continued to work to save America at the ballot box.

That reflects why I saw 2016 as the year of the New American Revolution. If Donald Trump had *not* risen victoriously to the top, I believe he would have stayed in the hard fight. This was a battle to take back America.

Donald Trump brought out voter support in numbers previously unseen.

Even in the 2016 Presidential Primary, with its ridiculous field of more than two dozen candidates, Republicans saw a record voter turnout. Many reported numbers up a full 50% over 2012. There seemed less interest in the Democrats' primary selection, with 20% lower voter turnout in 2016 over 2012. That struck me as peculiar.

In 2012, there should have been less turnout, since Barack Obama was simply running for re-election. In 2016, the field was open. Or, at least it seemed to be. In many eyes, if not for the Bernie Sanders factor, messing with her numbers and often beating her, most insiders simply assumed that Hillary Clinton would be the resounding choice.

Meanwhile, Donald Trump took on the powerful insiders of the Republican Party. He steadily beat out experienced, seemingly more qualified candidates. By the end of the Primary season, he landed more than 13 million votes, nearly 2 million *more* than the previous record, which had been set by George W. Bush.

For all his crass talk, voters did not disqualify Donald Trump for being just like (or frequently, not nearly as bad as) boys and men we've known all our lives.

Who hasn't heard construction workers whistle when a good-looking woman walks by? They are not whistling because they like her hat. Who hasn't heard men talk about women as sex objects, often including a number-scale ranking of 1 to 10.

The Bimbo Has *MORE* Brains

The old bar room joke comes to mind. "Keep drinking pal. She's a 2 at 10 but a 10 at 2."

In volume 1, **The Bimbo Has Brains... and Other Freaky Facts**, I discuss some of the very "bad boy" activities that have been tolerated in the White House. At least with Donald Trump, it's part of his past, rather than the garbage about Oval Office "rompings" we usually don't learn about till later.

Love him or hate him, but Donald Trump drew huge crowds to his rallies. Voters were so excited to see him that they often stood in long lines for up to 8 hours just to have that privilege. That reminds me of the crowds gathering overnight at ticket windows to be in line when concert tickets went on sale the next morning. (This was before the days of the Internet, of course.)

Hillary Clinton didn't draw the big crowds, but she was already a known political entity. She had polling data, media support, and her hard-earned infamy.

She'd worked for many years shoring up her stature as one of the most powerful and most hated women in America. I guess that's fair, because from what I observed, she hates men, and she can't stand women.

That said, voters may recall how quick the media was to play recordings of Trump's crass lingo. So, why did they downplay or totally ignore audiotape that revealed her disdain?

You may or may not recall hearing her laughing and scoffing that she'd gotten an alleged rapist of a 12-year-old girl "off" on a technicality. And she believed that he'd done the crime! She laughed. And Hillary Clinton wanted us to believe that she was the representative of women that we needed. Seriously.

I can't help but think that most of her votes had to have come from true devotees, if not dyed-in-the-wool straight-ticket Democrats. Even voters who did not like Trump knew they did not like Clinton either. And I am not even needing to touch the idiocy of her private server/classified email scandal. Nor do I need to dredge up her deadly debacle in mishandling Benghazi. Then there are is the Clinton Foundation, and all its controversy.

One thing seems to have been crystal clear to the American voters. There was a great fear of a continuing downward spiral for America if Hillary Clinton took the helm. 2016 truly was a revolutionary vote for either change or more of the same. Neither candidate had wowed anyone with likeability. However, voters merely needed to vote against Clinton, against more of the same, to hand Trump his decisive victory.

To vote against Hillary, some say that voters could have selected the Independent or Green Party candidates, instead of the crass "Trumpster." However, basic math shows that would be a vote for Hillary. That would have defeated the purpose.

Personally, I liked the Republican candidate Dr. Ben Carson, though I doubted that he could get enough traction or had the Chutzpah to become President. As an independent voter in New Hampshire, I got to choose either a Democrat or Republican ballot in the Primary.

For my taste, Republicans couldn't get enough egos out of the way to whittle their candidate numbers down ahead of time. However, I knew that a vote for Bernie Sanders *could* make a statement against Clinton on the Democratic ticket, even though he was not my favorite in the huge field of all Presidential hopefuls.

Though I would not have wanted a Communist or devote Socialist in the White House, I cast my vote against Hillary when I voted for Bernie Sanders in the New Hampshire Primary. I did it a second time by voting for Donald Trump in the General Election.

For me, it was a choice between unity and divisiveness… a choice between growth and regression, a choice between political favors and smart business policies. Saying this, I totally recognize that some people cast their vote for Hillary Clinton for the exact same reasons. As I said, I believe that most of us want the same results. We see different "right" routes to get there.

The Bimbo Has *MORE* Brains

As election results started coming in, I realized that winning the New American Revolution had not only been a possibility for Donald Trump, his team, and the millions of Americans who were desperate for change. It was now a probability.

Who'd have "thunk" it? Donald Trump, that's who... the unwitting leader of the New American Revolution.

Tip:
  "If you're walking down the right path, and you're willing to keep walking, eventually you'll make progress."
                                           -- Barack Obama (1961 -)
                                           44th President of the United States

18
Flashbacks

> *"There is nothing to fear except*
> *the persistent refusal to find out the truth."*
> -- Dorothy Thompson (1893-1961)
> American Journalist & Radio Broadcaster

As the political pendulum swings from right to left and from left to right, many years come and go. Policies change. Social mores shift. Even our political parties' platforms vary over the years. For example, one may be hawkish at one time and peaceniks at another.

Again, I have never been a fan of "party politics." I have opted instead to remain independent since first registering to vote in 1972.

But I have found it interesting over the years to observe how we humans label people based on political party affiliation. Even more interesting is how inaccurate these labels often are.

Started as one party against the Federalists, the Democratic Republican Party formed to support states' rights and followed a strict interpretation of the Constitution. They supported legislation favorable to family farms. They opposed elitism, as it reminded them far too much of England's monarchy. They stood against the Federal party, which wanted a national bank and priority given to the federal government and away from the states.

Infighting eventually caused them to split into two parties... Democrats and Republicans.

It may come as a surprise to many to learn that Democrats originally sought small government and wanted no interference from Washington. And since early in the 19th Century, the Republicans were the party that was all about rights for everyone, including Blacks, Indians, and women.

Then Republicans started seeking ways to limit the reach of the federal government. Meanwhile, the Democrats started seeking federal government solutions for all of society's ills.

The nation was in turmoil, and conflict was rampant.

Following the Civil War, support for Democrats grew quickly, thanks to a surge from white southerners, who were bitter from losing the war. There would be no peace, nor respect in our "hallowed halls" of Congress.

In fact, in the mid-1850's Democratic representatives brutally beat the new Republican Party's Charles Sumner with a cane... right on the floor of Congress... after he gave a passionate anti-slavery appeal. Shamelessly, the attackers boasted that they'd kill him next time.

Support for maintaining and expanding slavery, plus returning fugitive slaves, cost the Democrats votes. By 1860, the anti-slavery Republican Party had gained widespread popularity, and Abraham Lincoln became the first Republican President.

Sure, there were other issues, but how Congressional votes were cast is available for public knowledge. The 13th Amendment, to abolish slavery, passed in 1865 with 100% of Republicans voting for it, but only 23% of Democrats.

Republicans were first labeled "radical Republicans" during the Civil War, because they not only wanted an end to slavery, but they wanted to give slaves full citizenship, equality, and rights. Radical!

The 14th Amendment, giving full citizenship to freed slaves, passed in 1868. 94% of Republicans voted for it. Not one Democrat voted for it.

The 15th Amendment, giving freed slaves the right to vote, passed in 1870. 100% of Republicans voted for it. Not one Democrat voted for it.

Republicans stood for national unity and individual freedoms. Democrats fiercely opposed both.

The Ku Klux Klan was a powerful arm of the Democratic Party. It was designed to terrorize freed slaves and white Republicans dubbed as "nigger lovers" by Democrats.

History shows that such Republican thinking did not stop in the 1800's. Fast forward a Century. In the 1950's, Republican President Dwight D. Eisenhower integrated the U.S. Military and promoted civil rights for minorities. He also pushed through the Civil Rights Act of 1957. One of his most staunch opponents was a Democrat by the name of Lyndon B. Johnson, who was the Democrats' Senate Majority Leader at the time.

Congressional records show that Johnson consistently voted as a segregationist until he finally switched his position and voted for the Civil Rights Act of 1957. Even with his last-minute position change, there was still more support from Republicans, than from Democrats. Favorable votes went as follows.

House of Representatives	80% Republicans
	63% Democrats
Senate	82% Republicans
	69% Democrats

Thus, even 100 years after the parties split, Republicans were still the party of individual freedoms and anti-racism.

However, Democrats began employing an active campaign to *appear* as the party of hope for Blacks. In truth, the plan was purely designed to gain votes by creating federal financial support that would make minorities dependent on them... AND make them "forever supporters."

Clever politicking and smear campaigns, based on complete falsehoods, were born.

The parties did not "switch" their positions on these issues, as many want desperately to claim. I "get it." It's embarrassing in this day in age to accept painfully distasteful facts.

However, facts don't lie.

Remember, as Hillary Clinton re-quipped during her 2016 Presidential bid, "You are entitled to your own opinion, but not your own set of facts."

Voting records reveal actuality. Overt racists, like George Wallace, stayed strong in the Democratic Party.

Republican Barry Goldwater is sometimes touted as proof that the Republican Party is racist, because he was opposed to the Civil Rights Act of 1964. What we don't usually hear is what radio commentator Paul Harvey called "the rest of the story." Goldwater had opposed the Bill because of his advocacy of States' Rights versus Federal Law. He wanted to prevent the federal government from taking on all control over the individual states.

Still, the Democrats' active smear campaign worked, as ironically, in the 1964 Presidential election, Barry Goldwater lost in a landslide to an overt racist, Lyndon B. Johnson.

Because the scheme had worked, Democrats continued to falsely label Republicans as racists. They kept repeating it, and the media kept reporting it. So, today, people quite innocently tend to believe the clever political myth.

In actuality, racists existed then and now in BOTH political parties.

The myth is just another political lie. The myth created a public perception that then becomes "reality," even when there is no basis in "actuality" or fact.

A lie becomes perceived as truth because of repetition. Perception is accepted as reality, even when it's far from the truth.

In the 1960's, the Democrats saw they *had* to change their strategy. Because of "earlier Republican initiatives on Civil Rights, blatant racial oppression was no longer a viable political option."

The lack of logic is nothing new in politics. Look back at history and we find lots of examples.

In 1833, Seth Luther's "Address on the Right of Free Suffrage" addressed the plight of workers who didn't own land. Rhode Island's charter rules at the time stated that only land owners could vote. This lacked logic since the cities were growing, and people were leaving farms in droves to seek good jobs in the city.

Luther asked why 12,000 working people in Rhode Island were not being allowed to vote. Instead, they were being forced to submit to the will of the 5,000 people who owned land and, thus, could vote.

Let's fast forward again nearly 200 years to another scenario that lacks logic.

We've touched on this, but let's drill down to some details. As of November, 2017, nearly 128 million Americans had full-time employment. This means that they pay taxes. One way of looking at that is to note that their taxes pay for the lifestyle and benefits of those who do not work. Those numbers include some 95 million people, many of whom are retired, and have already paid their taxes. However, records show over 45-million people received food stamps in 2016. So, the 128 million are forced to pay for the lifestyles of the 45 million.

That sounds harsh. It's really not. I don't know anyone who doesn't agree with supporting people who are *unable* to work. As we've said, where folks start getting hot under the collar is when they know they are paying for so many people who *won't* work.

Unfortunately, when people get a taste of the benefits they receive when not working, they lack incentives to go back to work.

It's hard to know exactly how many of the 45-million people are capable of working, rather than truly unable to work. Several reports put the number of people who truly need and deserve assistance at around 20 million.

So, who are these other estimated 25-million people who will not work and prefer living off the taxes of hard-working Americans? Please note that I say, "<u>will</u> not work." I am not including those who have earned their retirement benefits from years of hard work. I am not talking about men and women who risk their lives in military service to this nation. I am not talking about children or elderly in need of the basic comforts of food, clean water, and a roof over their heads. I am not talking about people who truly physically cannot work.

I am talking about the millions who <u>won't</u> work, and who mistake their government-granted financial aid as something to which they are entitled… money and support they "deserve." Naturally, these millions of people continue to vote to elect politicians who promise to maintain their handouts and freebies. Politicos and entitlement-hungry people have actually started believing that the government pays for these billions in benefits.

The truth is that hard-working Americans pay for entitlements, often at the expense of their own lifestyles.

- Retired people often downsize, because once on a fixed income, they can ill-afford the ever-increasing tax burdens placed on them and their property.

- Working people can often no longer afford dental coverage or good health care insurance because they are paying so that non-workers can get full healthcare coverage at <u>no</u> cost, including dental services that these workers must pay toward on their own monthly bill. This seems twisted to me since these same workers can't afford dental coverage for themselves any longer.

- Young workers who secure an exciting job out of college get shocked at the huge proportion that has been taken out of their seemingly good salaries to pay taxes.

I grow tired of people saying they'd work if they could, but they can't find a *good* job. I never felt "above" starting at minimum hourly wage, which was a meager $1.60 for me. I was pleased when I'd get a 5-cent or 50-cent hourly raise. When merit raises turned annual salaries up by thousands, I was inspired to apply my good work ethic and work even harder.

I lack empathy for folks who simply don't want the cut in lifestyle that taking a job might cost them. Hello!?!

Try what the rest of us do... try working harder with a second or even third job. Try cutting back on the lifestyle pleasures that many workers cannot afford... even if it means dropping smoking, drinking alcohol, enjoying cable or satellite TV, or playing games on a smart phone.

Verbalizing such a reality won't win a politician votes from this burgeoning segment of the population. However, financially penalizing workers could eventually lead to dissolution of our American lifestyle and freedoms.

Let's be serious. Might it be more fair if people who <u>will</u> not work were not be entitled to vote on how to spend the money of people who <u>do</u> work? Woah! That's tough.

Howard Zinn, author of **A People's History of the United States**, notes that our 2-party system affords political leaders "an ingenious mode of control" over the masses. (p. 217; 2003; HarperCollins Publishers). This is so true. Keep feeding them, rather than teaching them to feed themselves and you maintain full control.

Some contend that everyone doesn't have equal means to enjoy "life, liberty, and the pursuit of happiness." Others argue that equal means should require equal effort.

As I understand is typical, when I was in college, I held different political feelings than I hold today. Toward the end of my bachelor's degree studies, I enjoyed an international internship in Copenhagen, Denmark. That summer experience dramatically opened my eyes and re-shaped my thinking. Most importantly, it gave me an extraordinary appreciation for the United States of America.

Most of us have no idea how truly fortunate we are to live here. And how *would* we know since we have nothing with which to compare it?

Copenhagen gave me a comparative model. Though an active, international seaport, it was also an extremely safe city. One of my fellow student interns, Kay, and I could walk around at any hour… without concern. Moms and Dads could both take time off following the birth of a baby and could then even alternate time off to share in the raising of young children. If someone took ill, as one of the gals staying in our flat did, we could dial two digits on the phone, and a doctor made an immediate house call… at no charge to us.

I was fascinated that a college education could be had… for free. Of course, for *me*, the age at which you had to take tests to determine your course of study options, would likely have qualified me to study "Gummy Bears 101" or the old stand-by, "Underwater Basket Weaving."

As the weeks in Denmark went by, I continued to observe. The food stores didn't yet have any package mixes. There were no "fast foods" available. You cooked from scratch, or you didn't cook at all. Frozen vegetables were brand new. I remember one supermarket featuring a square chest freezer with some miniature bags of frozen vegetables inside. It was their first freezer, so they proudly displayed it up front by the cash registers.

Flashbacks

Most homes did not have television sets. A few did. Others had a record player. Rarely did a home have both. For the World Cup soccer games, huge crowds gathered in the pedestrian walking streets, where numerous storefronts sported displays of televisions, all tuned to the games for the public to enjoy.

I learned about life in a free, yet socialized nation. Pricing and cost of living were dramatically different. For example, at the time, a new Volkswagen "bug" was selling in the U.S.A. for $3,000. The exact same car in Copenhagen was proudly advertised for the equivalent of "just" $15,000.

Gasoline prices had skyrocketed in the U.S.A. to 37-cents per gallon. The equivalent gallon cost in Denmark widened my eyes as it cost $1.50. Needless to say, I was glad to be able to walk or take the bus.

A sales tax was applied to every purchase. Luxury items got nailed with an additional 15% luxury tax. Okay, as college students we weren't in the market for a lot of luxury purchases, right? Wrong. Even such items as toilet paper were considered luxury goods. Oh, joy.

Then came the issue of income taxes. We were glad to be students, enjoying the lowest income tax bracket on our earnings... a mere 50%. This was 1974. Imagine the excitement here in the U.S.A. if they tried to take half your income as taxes, even while you were a student.

That said, I absolutely loved the people and the culture. I'd visit again in a blink.

However, learning and observing the political pros and cons... the costs and benefits of all the wonderful human services... gave me pause. There was something "off," though it took some time for me to put my finger on it. I talked a lot with managers and other people I met before I figured it out.

The Danes seemed very much like us, except kinder, gentler, friendlier, and more sexually relaxed.

What was it that was missing? I'll call it a "sparkle in their eyes." Fully socialized as a nation, there was no longer an opportunity for individuals to "get ahead" economically. Period.

I've observed this scenario many times since. For example, in London, a doctor lived in a third floor walk-up flat across the hall from a waiter. I'm not suggesting that a doctor is "better" than the waiter. However, from my cultural background in the USA, a doctor would make more money and keep more money than the waiter. In a socialized environment, everyone becomes somewhat "equalized." If you earn more, the government takes more.

I am unimpressed when very wealthy American politicians try to pretend or present themselves as relating to the everyday worker.

They only get away with that here because most Americans are unaware of a privileged societal layer called the Intelligentsia. Yet, we have most definitely got it.

I became very aware of the Intelligentsia back in the years of the Soviet Union… the U.S.S.R. Before covering President Ronald Reagan's Super Power Summit with Mikhail Gorbachov in Moscow as a television news journalist, I got to prepare at the nation's Russian Research Center at Harvard University.

There's nothing quite like gleaning information from our nation's leading Sovietologists to get ready for a whirlwind adventure behind the Iron Curtain. As Americans, we simply had no idea that beyond military prowess, the Soviet Union was very much what we would have considered to be a Third World Nation.

Let me try to deliver some perspective.

Just as we might grab a cold can of cola from a machine in public, citizens in Moscow could get their national beverage from a machine, too. They'd take the drinking glass off the machine's shelf and place it under a spigot. Put in your money and push a button, and the beverage filled the glass. Drink the beverage and place the glass back on the shelf for the next thirsty passerby. Okay, in all fairness, there actually was a "chemical wash" each user could opt to utilize between customers.

As my producer, videographer and I chronicled this slice of culture, we couldn't help but notice that the vast majority of patrons opted *not* to use the chemical wash. The reason? It made the beverage taste bad.

In Moscow, at the time, this meant such drinking glasses were potentially shared by some five-million people. Yet the nation's leaders wondered why the U.S.S.R. had one of the fastest increasing rates of infectious diseases in the world.

Hmmm. We aren't scientists, but we certainly knew one factor.

We are most assuredly spoiled in America. If we want to buy a car here, we go to any dealership and buy a car, often with financing options available on site. We can select a new or used car from a showroom floor or from a large array of vehicles on their lot. (Or nowadays, we can select from stock at virtually any dealership nationwide.) We can even order one with exactly the colors and specific options and extras we want.

In the Soviet Union, such options didn't exist back in the 1980's. If we had wanted a car, we'd have had to order a car and pay for it up front. We'd have had no choice of extras or even color. Simply enjoy your vehicle when it arrived… up to five years later.

The Soviet Union existed prior to the advent of cell phones, so hard-wired home telephones were still the standard. If we needed to have a phone installed, we could get it. Getting our phone number, however, was a lot tougher. There were no phone books. We simply had to create our own. How would we have learned our own phone number? When the phone rang, simply ask the caller what number they dialed. Perfect!

In the 1980's, we Americans were also in the process of infecting other nations, including the U.S.S.R., with some negative American habits. Astro Pizza, out of New Jersey, had just brought its first pizza truck to Moscow. Muscovites were loving it, but our "disposable mentality" was unknown to them. When folks came back to the truck to buy another take-out pizza, they brought the old box with them, not realizing they would get a fresh, new box.

Now, let me get back to the Intelligentsia. The Soviet Union made this an art form.

The average citizen waited up to 20 years for housing. This normalcy caused three generations to live together in most households. When a couple married, they immediately signed up for housing of their own, and moved in with parents on one side or the other. The hope was that by the time their children were grown, their names would have come up high enough on the list for their own housing.

I recall meeting a couple, not yet in their 30's, and their young son. Upon learning that this family already had their own housing, I immediately knew that they were part of the Intelligentsia. They were privileged… not because they or their parents had worked harder and saved more rubles… and not because they'd inherited a home or apartment… and not because they'd won a lucky lottery. Being in the Intelligentsia meant that they had the "right" connections with the "right" people in the reigning political regime.

These people got cars, while others waited years. They could go into restaurants otherwise restricted from use by Soviet citizens. They could own guns, though strict gun control laws made it totally illegal for civilian gun ownership, even for hunting.

Let me translate this into our all-American mindset. Let's say you are a high-ranking Democrat. When the Democrats are in power politically, you can have a better life, healthcare, buy a car, own guns and go hunting, and get an apartment. When the Republicans are in power politically, well-connected Republicans could have that lifestyle, and it would be taken away from you.

Anyone who has visited the Tower of London comes away with a much clearer perspective of our warped human foibles when it comes to politics. When one person lost the throne, that deposed ruler, their close family members, and their friends were apt to be immediately imprisoned... or worse. When they or their family *returned* to power, these people were released, and their enemies were imprisoned or killed. Back and forth it went.

Regardless of nation, those in power and their chosen circle of friends, family, and closest followers, get the privileged lifestyle. They are members of the Intelligentsia.

We have started to see this in the U.S.A. with increasing intensity in recent decades. If I am in power politically, I manage to find or develop cushy "jobs" for my cronies. Our challenge comes when I get out of office, and my cronies keep those jobs, along with everyone *they* hired. The newly elected person proceeds to find or develop cushy "jobs" for his or her cronies. It goes on and on, until we get to a point where nearly half the nation's workers seem to be employed directly or indirectly by the town, city, county, state, or federal government.

Oh, wait. We are there now. That's perhaps why we get so nervous when our Federal government has a "shutdown." We fear the loss of vital services, such as pay for military families. What we don't know are the facts.

In his January, 2017 syndicated column, John Stossel spelled it out. In a shutdown, all essential government workers stay on the job and continue to be paid. This includes military, along with "Law enforcement. Border patrol. The TSA. Air traffic controllers. The CDC. Amtrak. Power grid maintenance. Social Security checks. Medicare. Medicaid. Food stamps. Veterans hospitals. The U.S. Post Office. Federal courts. The EPA." And more.

Shutdowns are barely noticeable for most of us, other than the media hype they stir. Who even remembers the government being shutdown for 3 days under George H.W. Bush? Or for 16 days under Barack Obama? Or for 26 days under Bill Clinton?

There is no perfect society. There is no perfect way of dealing with us... we are imperfect people. There is no perfect form of government. Still, for all our weaknesses and woes, I like this little experiment called the United States of America... our Republic that loves Democracy... that respects and protects our individual rights... even when it can't protect us from ourselves.

The big political take-away I learned as a college student in Denmark was appreciation, awareness, and perspective. Since then, I have said that I wished that ALL our politicians on the national scene, particularly the lawmakers in the House of Representatives and Senate, lived elsewhere. I don't mean permanently, but for just, say, six months.

They could choose a free socialized nation, like England or Denmark. However, they could not take their U.S. assets with them. They'd need to live, work, and earn just as other citizens there do.

Then let them return to the U.S.A. and begin their term as a "public servant." I think it would be fascinating to see what legislation they'd then support and what rights they'd cherish... or revisit.

Tip:
> *"Free enterprise means that the more enterprising you are,*
> *the freer you are."*
>> --Mark Victor Hansen (1948 -)
>> American Author

19
Political Spectacles

"When you are wronged repeatedly, the worst thing you can do is continue taking it. Fight back!"
--Donald J. Trump (1946 -)
45th President of the United States

Personally, I am not very interested in politics. I dislike and distrust all politicians pretty much equally. As I mentioned, I have registered as an independent (undeclared, not to be confused with the Independent Party) since 1972, so I have from time to time been both a Democrat and a Republican following Primary elections.

I vote for people, not politicians or parties.

I know more than one smart woman who said, "I vow to vote against Hillary Clinton twice in 2016... first in the Primary and then in the General Election." When asked if there was anyone at all who could head the Republican ticket and cause her to change her mind, one replied, "I'd vote for Donald Duck before I'd vote for Hillary Clinton for anything."

She almost got her wish. She voted for a Donald after all.

Donald Trump rose up and won the Republican Party's nomination amidst harsh criticism from both liberals and leaders of his own party. He was not a flash-in-the-pan candidate who would implode the very next week. Okay, the next week. Okay, the one after that. He got in the 2016 race and ran it his way.

The public loved it. Some laughed. Some cheered. Some saw it as an entertainment. Some saw it as an opportunity for a completely new type of leader.

Whether they liked it or not, Republicans needed to recognize that Americans sought a new direction... a direction other than the standard Grand Old Party line... a direction that sung out loudly against political correctness... a direction that Donald Trump delivered. They hadn't even seen it coming.

Democrats also saw the Republic primary results through their own rose-colored glasses. They gleefully proceeded through to the general election anticipating Trump and his campaign to completely implode.

That did not happen. In fact, the groundswell blossomed and grew.

In the first weeks after Donald Trump became the Republican candidate in the 2016 Presidential race, even stunned Republicans stood numbed in disbelief that one of the more traditional candidates had not been able to overcome the political outsider. They could not fathom that the American people could not see what they purported and believed about Donald Trump.

From my perspective, I thought it disconcerting to see and hear otherwise smart Republican leaders defiantly making a spectacle of themselves. They did not want to remove their GOP blinders.

They could only see what they wanted to see, rather than what their constituents wanted to see.

I was reminded of words spoken by political activist and lecturer Helen Keller, the first person in the United States who happened to be deaf and blind and earned a Bachelor of Arts college degree. She aptly said, *"The most pathetic person in the world is someone who has sight, but has no vision."*

Donald Trump had his party's nomination, but he lacked their sincere support. Interestingly, he had captured a great deal of public support. The more criticism and accusations that were hurled at him, the more popular he seemed to become.

He'd never pretended to be holier than thou. He'd never trumpeted himself as being politically in "the know." He'd never tried to suggest that he'd not made a great many mistakes. Quite frankly, the fact that he'd been a very public person, with all his woes and victories "out there" for everyone to see for decades, made him a breath of fresh air.

Uphill battles are the stuff of which heroes and legends are made.

Neither party thought he'd come close to Democratic nominee Hillary Clinton in the General Election. Ooops!

Democrats couldn't believe that any Republican, but especially not Donald Trump could sweep through the nation and woo their traditional voters. This would be impossible. The philosophies and platforms of the Republicans were wrong, of course, and Donald Trump made them even worse. How could they possibly lose? He held hugely-attended rallies, but he must have been paying crowds of thousands to repeatedly show up… everywhere… Right?

Then it happened. In the general election, Hillary Clinton won more popular votes than Donald Trump, but he'd taken the heart of America, coast to coast.

"Fear grows in darkness;
if you think there's a bogeyman around,
turn on the light."
-- Dorothy Thompson (1893 – 1961)
American Journalist & Radio Broadcaster

"Not my President! Not my President!" Some California college students chanted defiantly following Donald Trump's defeat of Hillary Clinton. One gal that I saw interviewed said she was "heartbroken."

I ached for their hurt, but I knew they needed perspective. What only the wisdom of time would teach them is that the anger, frustration, fear, and pain *they* felt mirrored what the *other* half of their fellow citizens had felt when Barack Obama was elected... twice.

It mattered not. Barack Obama was President. Celebratory cheers of victory rose up. Tears of fear and disappointment also flowed.

Then Donald Trump turned the tables. This time, staunch liberals mourned the election results. Democrats had been so sure that they were electing the first woman to become President of the United States. They were confident that the wave of Obama popularity would carry Hillary Clinton to victory, even with people who didn't care for her personally.

So, was the disappointment because so many truly wanted to be able to vote for the first woman to become President? I have some dear friends that were so pleased to believe they had cast their votes in a manner that would prove that women had finally broken through the ultimate glass ceiling in the U.S.A. They felt genuine heartbreak when she lost.

Perhaps the overwhelming disappointment was due to an all-consuming fear over what some believed was going to be a Nazi, White Supremacist regime. Could there possibly be a fair-minded Trump administration?

Many had taken to heart the multitude of mass-media messages that had focused on some unsavory folks that were voting for Donald Trump and their philosophies, rather than on his philosophies.

> *"The great enemy of the truth is very often not the lie*
> *-- deliberate, contrived and dishonest --*
> *but the myth -- persistent, persuasive and unrealistic."*
> -- John F. Kennedy (1917 – 1963)
> 35th President of the United States

Personally, I like to vote for a person based on their quality. I do not expect all their politics to reflect all my views.

I cannot say that I was an early prognosticator of a Donald Trump victory. I hadn't initially thought he'd stay the Primary election course with the large field of Republicans and get the GOP's nomination. The American people know far more than I... as usual.

"There is no squabbling so violent as that between people who accepted an idea yesterday and those who will accept the same idea tomorrow."
-- Christopher Morley (1890 – 1957)
American Journalist

I will say that, as I looked back at the way the Primary season had unfolded, I was sickened by the words and actions of some people that I admired and greatly respected.

Mitt Romney, a man I had twice supported for President, broke my heart. When candidates had first started throwing their hats into the ring, I frequently commented that I did not believe he would go through those paces again. Yet, I believed he could be drafted at the Republican National Convention and stop the in-fighting. He'd been a Washington outsider who knew the sting of critics and a Republican leadership that had been reticent to leap to his side.

How soon we forget. Or, at least, how soon *he* forgot. How disappointing to watch Mr. Romney throw his words and money into fighting *against* a man that his fellow Republicans were backing in ever-increasing numbers.

And the Bush family seemed to do the same!

Why is it that politicians... from all parties... tend to forget that this nation was founded to be "for the people, by the people, and of the people?!?"

To *not* rally behind the people's choice – Donald Trump – shows a very short memory. Both Romney and Bush would have been appalled by any Republican leadership who didn't "fall in line," so to speak, when *they* were nominated.

Hmmm… how quickly a former Washington outsider – Mitt Romney – had become a seemingly insidious insider. I watched a good man behave badly. Very disappointing.

If anything, throwing money and opinion *against* Trump most likely drew more supporters *to* his camp.

We humans hate to have people tell us what to do, never mind how to think. That's part of what makes us tend toward being bad sports when things don't go the way we thought they would and should.

And we certainly saw bad sportsmanship (at best) and dangerous craziness (at worst) following the election of Donald Trump. American television personality Rosie O'Donnell is quoted as having wanted to see Marshall Law enacted… *anything* to prevent Donald Trump from taking office as President… and anything to keep Barack Obama in office. She said it was needed "until Trump is cleared of all charges."

Okay, there were no charges. Remember, we don't ever want to let facts get in the way of a good story. Charges? Was she on drugs?

I couldn't help but imagine how Democrats in Hollywood would have cried, "Foul" had Republicans tried to block Barack Obama from taking office in 2008.

Who can call themselves fair or open-minded when they protest against a President and call for his impeachment *before* he's even taken office? Hello! That smacks of immaturity and sour grapes. The 2016 election was over, and I thought that then we would get to learn what Donald Trump was like and see what sort of President we now had. He served up lists of cabinet appointees far more rapidly than his predecessors, and they included some highly qualified and successful individuals. This most assuredly would boost Trump's credibility as he surrounded himself with those who would serve as his most trusted advisors.

Unless people relied on television news commentaries to form their opinions, the Trump cabinet confirmation hearings inspired confidence. Listening to these people handle the questions thrown at them was fascinating and inspiring. Good for Donald Trump for choosing them as his core team of senior advisors and leaders for the nation's highest posts.

However, the political divisiveness was just heating up.

New Jersey Democratic Senator Cory Booker ranted against Alabama's Republican Senator Jeff Sessions during his Senate Confirmation Hearings to join Trump's Cabinet as Attorney General. He sounded far less like someone trying to ascertain Sessions' fitness for the Cabinet post than someone seeking a 2020 Presidential bid for himself. Even after much testimony that clearly demonstrated Sessions' fair-mindedness and extraordinary work for minority rights, Booker's campaign-like monologue resounded with baseless accusations that Sessions "had not demonstrated a commitment to justice for *all.*"

I would think that if I have strong concerns regarding a President-elect, then I would want to surround him with truly good people. Counterproductivity to slow or halt the process and crush anyone and everyone who might associate with Donald Trump seemed way over the top and self-defeating.

Combative is a far cry from Progressive. Thankfully, not all Progressives are actually Regressives. In fact, while peaceful protest is worthy, respectable, and valuable, the "Trumped" up "outrage" became downright Regressive. Plain and simple.

For great examples of this, we need only look at the mayhem in 3rd World nations. Watch the video taken at foreign protests where people *cheer* when someone murders an opposing candidate or their supporters. Yikes!

This most definitely reflects backward, uncivilized thinking.

Still, leading up to our 2017 Presidential Inauguration Day, we saw repeated examples of people negatively pressuring others for having been invited to take part in the great American tradition.

Protests are fine. Bravo. Personally, I like protests that show courage. With regard to politics, I smile when people stand up to bullying.

I do recognize the Regressives, these faux-Progressives, as bullies. They are dividing the Democrats just as hard-lined GOP leaders were dividing the Republicans.

I stated in the earlier chapter, the "would-be Progressives" who tried like mad to get elected officials, celebrities, and even school marching bands to boycott the US Presidential inauguration were bullying people. Great democratic thinking... not.

Because we hate that Hillary lost, and we can't believe America voted for Donald Trump, let's boycott. Let's force *others* to boycott, too. Let's prevent high school and college kids from having a once-in-a-lifetime opportunity to take part in one of the most amazing parts of what makes America great... the peaceful transfer of power. You know... inauguration... the time when partisan politics take a holiday, and we celebrate our nation's liberty.

Since so many liberals felt driven to protest vehemently after Trump's election, perhaps our days of democracy are numbered. I prefer not to think so.

However, it was interesting to see the Boomerang Bullying effect at work again. With fascination I watched protests end up garnering *more* support for Donald Trump.

Why should artists, celebrities, designers, entertainers, and even high school and college marching bands be subjected to so much flak from their peers or anyone else? This is a real "bee in my bonnet." If someone gets invited to perform at a Presidential Inauguration, "Congratulations" is the right thing to say. Only political bullies would say, "Don't you dare!"

Hmmm… to me, badgering anyone, from actors to singers, to *not* perform because *I* don't care for someone's politics smacks of bullying and harassment. Whether it's politics, business, or sex, people are getting "Weinsteined," and it must stop.

Political badgering and shaming is bullying, just as the sexual harassment and assault mess is bullying!

You may recall that the talk and verbal pressures deepened as groups threatened extreme violence in Washington, D.C. during the inauguration of President Trump. Then I heard about a group called "Bikers for Trump," some 200,000 members strong. Thousands of them headed to Washington to defend the Donald Trump inauguration against groups that vowed to bust up the inauguration.

Chris Cox, the group's leader, said they would "form a wall of meat." They planned to stand "shoulder to shoulder with their brothers and go toe to toe with anyone who breaks through police lines and tries to assault anyone."

He added that they "want to be sure that people who came to watch and celebrate the peaceful transition of power get the opportunity to do so."

I also learned a lot about human nature as I watched elitists exude so much energy putting down Donald Trump's inauguration concert choices, as if these were somehow sub-par and, thus, scoffingly reflective of how classless they think Donald Trump is.

Hmmm… These folks showed who was clueless, tasteless, low class, and disrespectful. Though not what they anticipated, however, their "not-so-progressive" spotlight illuminated themselves, rather than their intended target.

This is "Boomerang Bullying."
Bullies try to control or put someone down,
but the negative smacks *them*, not their target!

How could the American public <u>not</u> grow tired of the endless complaining and deliberate concoction of false concepts in attempts to stir unrest. Pooh-poohing is one thing, but the constant condescension over his decisions revealed far more about the mud-throwers than about Donald Trump.

To his credit, long-time American journalist, Geraldo Rivera, reminded TV viewers that when John F. Kennedy beat Richard Nixon, election information came out that showed vast numbers of truly illegitimate votes had been cast for Kennedy by people who'd been dead for years. Nixon supporters called for election fairness and reform, but they did not riot, rant and rave, or try to stop Kennedy's inauguration. They respected our nation and the process, despite the genuine flaws that may have cost their candidate the White House.

In 2016, the name-calling crowd grew louder, as if yelling would make false words true. However, *calling* Donald Trump and his supporters Fascists, racists, and misogynists doesn't make it *true*.

Months after the election, we continued to hear some liberals encouraging people to *continue* the rant against Trump. As irony would have it, this only seemed to make Trump's popularity go up and bolstered his supporters' commitment and resolve.

What is with our great American desire to point the finger of blame at anyone other than ourselves?

Barack Obama had put down Fox News throughout the 8 years that he was President. Despite President Obama's popularity, Fox News ratings continued to go up, not down.

Hillary Clinton wrote a book attempting to explain what went wrong that caused her to lose the election. Instead of being angry that she lost, she perhaps should consider that she lost public trust by her own highly questionable actions.

Regardless of whether or not you are a Hillary Clinton fan, you had to have cringed during the investigation into her use of that unsecured, private server. When asked if she'd "wiped the server," she literally tried to play the unwitting innocent. Insulting is the best thing I can say about her response, "You mean like with a cloth?"

Donald Trump has made us all cringe, too. More than once his off-the-cuff Tweets came off as just too plebian for a President. We cringed. We wished he would apply his smarts and business savvy in his social media communications.

However, Donald Trump held his ground. He is what he is and makes no apology for it. I actually like that.

Many members of the media put Trump down for labeling a CNN reporter "rude" for yelling over Trump's attempt to field a question from a different reporter. Then he labeled the reporter a proponent of fake news. No journalist wants to hear *that*. Then again, no journalist should yell at a President.

The Bimbo Has *MORE* Brains

Like it or not, Donald Trump fights back. That makes most of us smile. He creates spectacles to watch.

Kellyanne Conway, Counselor to the President, also noted that Donald Trump rarely draws first blood. But he does fight back. President Trump says he is glad to have the "microphone" to stand up to bullying, because most people don't get such a microphone. In a fascinating way, he often gives us… the little guys… hope.

We saw him do it again when he backed Linda Bean, the granddaughter of the L.L. Bean founder. She's not one of "the little guys," but she was most assuredly getting bullied. Liberals had encouraged boycotts against her business interests because she had supported Donald Trump with a campaign contribution to a pro-Trump political action committee.

It made me smile to see L.L. Bean sales go *up*, despite the national boycott. Boomerang Bullying! Again!

Thank you, Donald Trump! It's rather nice to have someone fight back on behalf of America, especially middle America. We are not all sharp, sophisticated city folks, nor ultra-cultured consumers, nor multi-millionaire celebrities. Most of us are simply normal, day-to-day, hardworking, typical Americans.

Interestingly, while some people focused on how they could block Donald Trump from becoming President, and then on how they would stop him from getting anything accomplished, especially in his first 100 days, Donald Trump simply got to work. Unlike those who came before him, he would not get the traditional Presidential "honeymoon."

Where was the outrage by critics when, barely a week after the election, comedians and celebrities found it perfectly suitable to openly mock and imitate our new First Lady, Melania Trump, during the 2016 American Music Awards telecast, no less. Was this beauty-shaming? Was it immigrant-shaming? Or were they merely showing their disrespectful ignorance by thinking they were humorous?

Hmmm... Just imagine the outrage had such a thing been done to Mrs. Obama at any time during Barack Obama's White House tenure. Imagine again if it had happened before her husband had even been sworn in as President?

Despite efforts to disrupt the process, between his election and Inauguration Day, Donald Trump accomplished a lot more than we might expect to hear from mainstream media. He's officially on record as having done more to stop Government interference in our lives in his first 100 days than any other President in history.

This included signing 13 resolutions that rolled back unnecessary regulations and blocked agencies from reissuing them. The first 100 days included him signing 30 Executive Orders, as compared with President Johnson's 26, President Kennedy's 23, President Truman's 20, President Eisenhower's 20, President Obama's 19, and Ronald Reagan's 18.

Despite naysayers trying to claim that President Trump can't work with Congress, he managed to work with lawmakers in the first 100 days to enact more legislation than any President since Harry Truman. The Trump Administration enacted 28 laws, as compared with President Kennedy with 26, President Clinton with 24, Presidents Eisenhower and Carter with 22 each, President George H.W. Bush with 18, and President Obama with 11. No one has come close to President Truman's record of 55.

We hear lots about "internal chaos." Supposed "tell-all" books are instant best-sellers, as we humans hunger for "dirt."

We probably should be hearing about at least a few of the 100+ accomplishments since Donald Trump was elected President.
- 1.7 million new jobs were created and unemployment dropped to 4.1%, its lowest level since 2007.
- Billions of dollars in corporate reinvestment in America.
- Added $500-million in SBA loans for women-owned businesses.
- The stock market has repeatedly hit new record high levels.
- Gross Domestic Product (GDP) rose 3%.

- The Consumer Confidence level rebounded to a 17-year high at 125. (This is a number that can fluctuate dramatically, as seen with President Obama who hit a low of 25 in his first year in office and a high of 113.)
- Got his promised tax reform bill passed, slashing $5.5-billion in taxes.
- Won approval of his Supreme Court nominee Neil Gorsuch.
- Ended the Obamacare mandate that requires everyone to have health insurance or be fined.
- Declared a nationwide Public Health Emergency on opioids and added $500-million to help fight the crisis.
- Signed several Acts to better support Veterans and authorized over $2-billion in additional funding.
- Directed rebuilding and strengthening of the military.
- Won the release of Americans being held abroad.
- Made good on a campaign promise to recognize Jerusalem as the capital of Israel.

The Trump Administration did all this despite worsening political infighting. Whether he'd been elected more because people liked his hot agenda topics or because they couldn't stand Hillary Clinton mattered little.

Now we had a very effective President, despite being fought against and slowed down by his own political party, which held the Congressional majority. Republicans were guaranteeing that his agenda would, at least, be mired in political muck. Interestingly, members of his own party seemed to frequently be working against President Donald Trump.

> *"There are times in politics*
> *when you must be on the right side and lose."*
> -- John Kenneth Galbraith (1908 – 2006)
> Canadian Economist & Diplomat

President Trump was undaunted. He shook his head and, being the studied businessman that he is, he continued to negotiate and plan and work to achieve what the nation had made clear was wanted.

He suffered setbacks on some of his agenda items, but he has enjoyed far more successes, all within just a year after being elected.

I heard the following after the 2012 Presidential election, lost for the second time by Mitt Romney to Barack Obama.

* * * * * * * * * * *

A union shop foreman walks into a bar next door to the factory and is about to order a drink to celebrate Obama's victory when he sees a guy close by wearing a 'Romney for President' button and two beers in front of him. He doesn't have to be an Einstein to know that this guy is a Republican. So, he shouts over to the bartender so loudly that everyone can hear, "Drinks for everyone in here, bartender, but not for that Republican."

Soon after the drinks have been handed out, the Republican gives him a big smile, waves at him, then says, "Thank you!" in an equally loud voice. This infuriates the Union captain. The Union captain once again loudly orders drinks for everyone except the Republican. As before, this does not seem to bother the Republican. He continues to smile, and again yells, "Thank you!"

The Union foreman, for a third time, loudly orders drinks for everyone except that Republican. As before, the Republican continues to smile, and again yells, "Thank you!"

The Union guy finally asks the bartender, "What the hell is the matter with that Republican? I've ordered three rounds of drinks for everyone in the bar but him, and all the silly idiot does is smile and thanks me. Is he nuts?"

"Nope," replies the bartender, "He owns the place."

* * * * * * * * *

Tip: In politically challenging times, remember the words of singer/songwriter Jimmy Buffet who said, "Thank God we're crazy or we'd all go insane."

20
We've Got Issues

> *"I am a woman above everything else."*
> -- Jacqueline Kennedy Onassis (1929 – 1994)
> First Lady; Wife of 35th President of the United States

American comedian Loni Love (1970 -) quipped, "I like Condoleezza Rice. She's a smart woman. She knows four or five languages. Plus her name sounds like a side dish at Kentucky Fried Chicken."

Not sure how this comic bit strikes you. It raises an eyebrow for me, as it sounds like a deliberately back-handed compliment. Because a black woman said it, today's protocol dictates that we should not criticize. Regardless, I know that if a man had said this, we'd wince openly.

I am equally sure that a white comedian making cutesy, put-down quips about a strong black woman, say Michelle Obama, would get slammed. Critics would be up in arms even if the comedian had included that they liked Mrs. Obama and that she is smart.

We've lost our way.

We've gotten creepily hyper-sensitive. However, it's only politically correct to be sensitive to one side.

Whenever we touch on issues, we step on toes.

For example, John Ridley, was quoted on the topic of abortion. "I'm not saying whether abortion is right or wrong. I'm just saying I'm a man. I know men. And I'll tell you right now, if men could get pregnant, not only would abortions be legal, I think McDonald's would be doing them."

It matters little that Ridley was born in 1965 and raised in Wisconsin by successful, hard-working parents. It matters little that Ridley is a black man. It matters little that Ridley is an Academy Award-winning American screenwriter and film director.

What does matter is that the abortion topic is a hot potato. He has every right to express his opinion. However, paralleling abortion's would-be popularity with drive-through fast food, kicks our human divisive mode into high gear. Whether it should or shouldn't, it does.

Why is the day that we do laundry, cook, clean, run errands, and so on, called a day *off*?

So many issues are hot potatoes today. In the 1980's, I first started hearing that we needed healthcare reform. I believed then and now that we have the finest healthcare in the world. What we needed then... and now... is healthcare *insurance* reform. To my thinking, that is an industry that has taken ridiculous advantage of the political climate to drain money out of *our* pockets and the coffers of many employers.

First, they made insurance unaffordable. Then, in *their* brilliance, our politicians made it mandatory. And insurance companies made new policies that covered less for more money, with higher co-pays and consumer contribution portions. Great!

Oh, and if the soaring costs made it impossible to keep dental insurance, we could drop that. However, as we've said, we'd still find a monthly dental payment on our insurance bill to pay for dental coverage for *other* people who can't afford dental insurance.

Thanks! It made little sense. If I can't afford it for myself, it certainly won't please me to pay for someone else to have what I can't even afford for myself.

When I must choose between paying my mortgage or paying my health insurance, I guess I have to risk getting fined for not having health insurance. The Affordable Health Care Act... aka Obamacare... or the UN-affordable Health Care Act... crushed millions of hard-working American citizens. It will take years to get that sorted out. I seriously doubt pricing will ever get rolled back to logical, affordable levels.

> *"The doctor of the future will give no medicine but will interest his patients in the care of the human frame, in diet, and in the cause and prevention of disease."*
> -- Thomas Edison (1847 – 1931)
> American Inventor

Another issue that gets us riled up is the increasing violence in our society. We don't have to be involved in a war somewhere to feel this either. Internal discord has gotten out of control. While I applaud civil disobedience, I abhor violence.

When people use their power, strength, and smarts to hurt other people, we all lose.

Just months after taking office in the midst of ongoing war and increasing social upheaval, racial division, and political discord, President Donald Trump addressed the nation. Among his comments on August 21, 2017 he said, "There is no room for prejudice, no place for bigotry, and no tolerance for hate. The young men and women we send to fight our wars abroad deserve to return to a country that is not at war with itself at home. We cannot remain a force for peace in the world if we are not at peace with each other. Let us find the courage to heal our divisions within. Let us make a simple promise to the men and women we ask to fight in our name, that when they return home from battle, they will find a country that has renewed the sacred bonds of love and loyalty that unite us together as one."

Of course, following the address, most members of the media ignored his calls for unity. They focused on the fact that for years prior to running for President, Donald Trump was a staunch proponent for getting our military out of Afghanistan. In this address, he duly noted that fact, plus he detailed how his team had helped him shift his position to one that will not let our sacrifices of life and treasure be for nothing, since departing would leave a void that noted terror organizations would fill immediately.

Instead, President Trump spoke of how he has empowered our military leaders and is providing them with the tools they need to win.

He added, "Our troops will fight to win. *We* will fight to win. From now on, victory will have a clear definition... Attacking our enemies, obliterating ISIS, crushing Al Qaida, preventing the Taliban from taking over Afghanistan, and stopping mass terror attacks against America before they emerge."

He was perfectly clear on his feelings about terrorism, stating, "Terrorists who slaughter innocent people will find no glory in this life or the next. They are nothing but thugs and criminals and predators and – that's right – losers."

What about domestic terrorism? With the emergence of counter-protestors to protestors, our right to peaceful dissent is being twisted and challenged.

Detractors want to pound their chests and utter, mournfully, that President Trump didn't speak out quickly enough against the vile behavior in the clash of protestors and counter-protestors over the removal of a statue of Confederate General Robert E. Lee in Charlottesville, VA in 2017.

In truth, his message was very clear. Hatred and violence will not be tolerated.

What some did *not* like is the fact that President Trump recognized that hatred and violence was being perpetrated on *both* sides.

White nationalists had planned a protest at the park where the controversial statue was to be removed. No violence was planned. I am not saying that these folks were smart. I mean, they were going to be waving lots of Confederate flags. Brilliant. But it is their right.

Upon learning of the planned event, ultra-leftist groups spent weeks setting plans in motion to challenge them, and, yes, *these* plans included violence. They studied and targeted ultra-right leaders of the upcoming rally. Some arrived wearing helmets and masks and brandishing batons. One group wore black military gear and carried rifles. Many threw bricks and even Molotov cocktails at the rally goers. Some even pepper-sprayed them.

Naturally, word had gotten through to the protestors that these militant groups were rallying to protest their protest. They were *not* coming to be calm, rational counter-protestors, as the media reported. In other words, they were *not* coming to see the Robert E. Lee statue in the park end game. They were intending to "take on" the protestors, who most people recognized as ultra-racists.

Did the "radicalists" think the racists would just lay down and give up?

Not likely. They armed themselves with shields; some had guns.

Are both sides to blame? Of course. This was never going to be a peaceful sit-in once two sides were planning to clash. Protestors said they wanted "unity." That is bogus. Hello. Remember, they carried Confederate flags and chanted white supremacist lingo. That is just plain divisive.

This nation already has an enormous history of battling ultra-leftist thinking from our Civil War. People from the North typically have never understood the KKK and today's remnants, because the Union won, and the nation remained one.

Many people from the South never quite got past "losing" that war, and they still carry a certain bigotry and prejudice forward to future generations against those "damn Yankees." And they are not talking baseball.

Many claimed that some officials, if not "wanting" a violent Charlottesville event, acerbated the situation and inflamed the volatility of two clashing extremist groups. One report shows a police officer laughing as a protestor was sprayed with mace in the face by a counter-protestor.

Both sides came ready for a fight. Both sides point the finger of blame at the other side. Both sides struck out violently against the other. Both sides caused and sustained injuries.

Our right to peaceful protest was upheld. We have no right to violent protest, no matter how vile we see the cause of the other side as being.

For a moment, imagine that your friend James was at the park, thinking he was there for a peaceful protest… or counter-protest. Then imagine James getting separated from his friends and finding a crush of angry people screaming him down for his beliefs. He rushes to escape, but they keep holding him back and hitting him, also throwing bricks at him.

Finally, he manages to get to his car, but the assault doesn't stop. He tries to drive away from the chaos, but they stay with him, some hitting his car with their clubs. James finally gets away from the center of the mob, but he still feels bricks hitting his car. His panic and self-preservation push him… hard. He accelerates, though escaping through the crowd means mowing them down. Several are injured, and one young woman dies.

Did he mean to kill someone? I highly doubt it. Emotions and tempers blew quickly out of control… on both sides. With some 3-dozen people injured, from both sides of the conflict, the focus lands on the one death. To me, this parallels the inflammatory nature of the entire event.

At a peaceful protest, not one person should be threatened, never mind injured or killed. When violence breaks out on both sides, both sides *are* to blame, even when the tragedy of death was caused by only one of those sides.

One peaceful rally-goer's sign said it all: "Tolerance does not mean tolerating intolerance." Too bad that meaning was lost on both sides.

KKK, Nazis, and other white supremacists may be utterly despicable in my view and the view of others. However, to *them*, they were protecting what they see as America's moral values… just as the counter-protestors were protecting what *they* see as America's moral values.

"Yikes," you may say. I agree.

We, as humans everywhere, have always existed in direct dichotomy with other humans' philosophies. This is not purely American. This is purely human.

We do not want Republicans to embrace racists and other right-wing extremists. Nor do we want Democrats to embrace racists and other left-wing extremists. Yet, we quickly point the finger at leaders of both Parties because some wacko group likes them.

Why must we politicize everything so vehemently? Critics quickly rejected President Trump's criticism of protestors and counter-protestors for getting things out of control. Had these critics sincerely believed this or any other President would have been cheering such abhorrible events?

Why can't we all recognize that <u>all</u> extremists present issues of danger? For example, the socialist, extreme leftist group, Antifa, hides themselves in masks, reflecting their KKK roots. So, they hide their personal identities while they beat and abuse conservatives or anyone else who disagrees with them. Whenever I see protestors of any sort hiding their own identities with scarves or masks, I recognize that they are not true believers in their cause.

> *"I do not want the peace that passeth understanding. I want the understanding which bringeth peace."*
> -- Helen Keller (1880 – 1968)
> American Activist

We can also look at our environmental challenges and stir up all sorts of ire. We can all learn from lessons that teach us to take everything we can from life, but to always remember from where we took it.

Humans are the only species who cut down trees, make paper from it, and then write on the paper: "Save the Trees."

Climate change. Global warming. Global cooling. These cycles have been going on for eons... literally.

Though it became popular in certain circles to blame President George W. Bush for everything, he didn't invent global warming any more than Al Gore invented the Internet. (Sorry, I realize that you likely need to be from a certain generation for that slice of sarcasm.)

Has our modern day industry hastened global warming? Likely. Scientists admit, however, that we won't have accurate measurements of any impact until well after the fact.

Logic tells us that if we are spewing toxins into the atmosphere, it is apt to negatively impact the atmosphere. Even if the results turn out to be minimal or negligible, trying to minimize poisonous emissions won't do any harm. Such steps may help.

In truth, scientists acknowledge one fact about such emissions that we haven't heard about from the media, mainstream or otherwise. Our rapidly expanding worldwide population may have a great deal more to do with adversely impacting climate change than factories and automobiles spewing waste into the atmosphere. This is caused by the carbon dioxide released through the skin and breathing of every human being's body. The daily noxious levels from one single adult human have been noted as worse than those from the exhaust of a big ol' gas-guzzler automobile, such as the Galaxy 500. Yikes!

Now let's look at horrific storms and other cataclysmic events. Take 2017's hurricanes, for example. Harvey, Irma, and José alone devastated islands and the US mainland, destroying billions of dollars' worth of property and causing tragic loss of life from the Caribbean to Florida and Texas. Houston, Texas had already suffered one of the most horrific floods.

Then California's wine country and southern California suffered the violently vicious effects of multiple wildfires, torching hundreds of acres of land, turning entire neighborhoods to ash, and rapidly snuffing out human life. 2016 had seen dramatic, fast-moving fires in both North Carolina and Tennessee mountains. In 2017 a massive earthquake racked Mexico City. The island of Bali suffered back-to-back volcanos within just days of each other. On the day after Christmas in 2004, nearly a quarter of a million people lost their lives when a giant tsunami slammed several countries in Southeast Asia.

Some say that global warming is causing such events or at least causing them to be far worse than they would be otherwise. When we do a little fact checking on geology and our weather patterns, we see other aspects coming into play. For example, meteorologists note that weather follows cycles. Storms had been less intense for about a decade. The calm has been subsiding. Remember cycles they call "El Niño" and "Le Niña" making news? Well, here we go again. We will be hit and hit hard.

Storms will be more severe. Winds will be higher. Droughts will be tougher. Downpours will be more torrential.

Further, science has greatly improved technology for recording storm data now than previously. This helps us more quickly warn people in a storm's path. We also have better construction that increases the odds of buildings withstanding storms. Still, with all that our scientists know, we can't (yet) prevent or weaken storms.

Other catastrophes, like earthquakes, their resulting tsunamis, and volcanos don't follow predictable patterns. The planet's heating, cooling, and the shifting of its inner layers are studied by scientists, but not caused by humans or our industrialization.

Former NASA climatologist, James Hansen, thinks we could see a 10-foot rise in our ocean levels before the year 3000. In the August 13, 2015 issue 1241 of Rolling Stone, he was interviewed in the article "The Point of No Return" by Eric Holthaus. Hansen said, "Social disruption and economic consequences of such a large sea-level rise could be devastating. It's not difficult to imagine that conflicts arising from forced migrations and economic collapse might make the planet ungovernable, threatening the fabric of civilization."

We can wring our hands. We can march in protests. We can legislate for kinder industrial emissions.

We cannot control Mother Nature. We cannot stop climate change… no matter how many nations gather together in sincere discussions. We can and need to be kinder to our planet, but we should never misunderstand that environmental soundness is no match for natural cycles.

And, no. The storms and fires are not the fault of Donald Trump. Or George W. Bush. Or any other one individual.

Speaking of things that seem out of whack, let's look at crime and gun control. I totally "get it" that criminals will always be able to acquire any level of weaponry that they can afford. Making certain weapons illegal for law-abiding citizens to own assuredly keeps them <u>only</u> in the hands of the "bad guys," since they are perfectly willing to acquire weapons illegally. I "get" all that.

However, I also "get" that time after time, tragedy after tragedy, mass murder after mass murder, many assailants purchased *their* weapons *legally*.

Worse yet, many perpetrators have been previously "known to police" and even under investigation by authorities. We may prevent some, but obviously, not all heinous attacks displaying man's inhumanity to man.

I've never understood why someone thought it was justifiable to commit murder, especially in protest of acts they consider to be murder. We can work to make these actions illegal, if that is the result we seek. However, shooting revelers to death in a night club as a protest against bombing in Syria is ludicrous. Walking into a health clinic and shooting people or murdering a doctor equally defies rational logic.

We only show our weakness when we use some ideological or political vent as our angry rationale for grotesque actions. To bomb or shoot unarmed people... in a movie theatre... at church... in a night club... at a restaurant... wherever... similarly defies rational logic. Are the angry people who do these things sick, or are they sickos? Probably a combination.

It's far from easy to come up with political or legal solutions that don't trample on citizen's rights. It's even more impossible to legislate logical thinking. Being angry is not against the law. Taking anger out on other people or even their property is illegal.

When investigations show someone tends toward anger or imbalance, there is little that authorities can do without changing the U.S.A. into some totalitarian state. You can't arrest someone for having a negative attitude.

It's an impossibly tough balance to protect innocent, unarmed people while also protecting personal rights and freedoms. We want to be safe, but we are uncomfortable with the trade-offs that are likely required to guarantee safety from terrorist acts.

Where we all lose is when politicians or even media types stir up anger and "spit" at those who think differently, trying to paint them as being out of touch. This is definitely one of many issues on which everyone actually agrees on the desired outcome… protecting individual rights while protecting individuals and maintaining our American freedoms.

Work together politicos, and flush the name calling. It matters not whether someone calls themselves a Republican or a Democrat, any and every solution is going to please some people and annoy other people. Stand *together* and get over worrying about who gets the credit for being "right." I am not alone when I say that I am tired of accusations flying back and forth about which party is trying to block getting the job done. Phooey!

The "anger" factor has also been rearing its ugly head in an ugly manner of late whenever it comes to our dearly held freedom of speech.

But I still need to pose a question. When did *my* freedom of speech become more important than *your* freedom of speech? You know… if I don't like what you are saying at some town or school meeting, I should just scream my opinion louder than you or interrupt you by calling you names… anything so you can't talk and make your point. No? Oh. Of course, that's not right.

I also find it wrong when people try to interrupt or scream down some political candidate or representative who's giving a speech. Do I have a right to disagree? Yup. Do I have a right to speak my views? Yup. But I do not think I have the right to step on someone *else's* rights. By interfering with someone who is scheduled to speak, I would be treading on respectful people or anyone in attendance to hear that talk.

Actually, if I don't like a particular candidate, or I don't like the opinion I think they will be expressing, I have lots of choices, like:

- Don't go to the event.
- Don't vote for them.
- Go to the event and join or form a legal, peaceful protest.

If I think my position is far more valid, I could plan my own speech. Heck, I could run for political office, too.

If I choose angry actions or step on others' rights to try to get my opinion out, I am no better than the voice or opinion I am wishing to squelch.

I, for one, was sickened by the 2016 U.S. Presidential race when I saw various protestors screaming at and trying to intimidate a candidate's supporters. I don't care if they were hired protestors or genuinely distraught. They were behaving in a manner that I consider to be totally un-American and completely unacceptable. And woe to the whiners who belly-ached when someone actually responded to their belligerence in kind… with anger.

Did they think people would simply say, "Oh! You feel so violently angry on this subject, that you must be right. Thank goodness you enlightened me. I was a totally misguided person until you ranted and raved in my face. Yikes. I almost thought it was okay to have and even express a different opinion."

Having different opinions makes us stronger. Otherwise we might fall into a trap of just blindly believing what some political leader kept repeating. Now that would truly be reflective of an early Adolf Hitler strategy to form and force public opinion in his favor.

While I'm getting into trouble here, let me leap into another fray.

Economics is always a sticky wicket. Some of us want the government to do more. Some of us wish the government would be comprised of a smaller group and leave us alone. Regardless, a tidbit that a lot of us miss is the fact that the government doesn't really make money.

When someone says, "The government should pay for this or that," they are really saying that the workers should keep less of what they earned to *enable* the government to pay for this or that.

The difference that our tax structure has made on this nation is remarkable. We will never again see the unimaginable wealth of families, such as the Vanderbilts.

One need only visit our nation's largest single family residence to see what I mean. Though a museum today, The Biltmore in Asheville, North Carolina blows doors off even the wealthiest of homes, especially when we remember life at the time it was built. It was built before income and property taxes carved enormous chunks out of earnings.

It's boggling to imagine that just building The Biltmore spawned the entire city of Asheville, initially, just in support of this extreme 250-room "home."

One might argue that no home needs hundreds of acres, or 43 bathrooms, or 35 guest rooms and family rooms, or a 40-foot-long dining table in a banquet hall with a 70-foot-high ceiling. This is not to mention having its own dairy farm, stables, commercial-sized greenhouse, vineyard, and winery.

Okay. But George Vanderbilt created it because it suited his extravagant bachelor lifestyle, and then became his family home. The public now benefits from the fact that his heirs could not support the crazy high taxes. They donated thousands of acres of land to be protected, and they opened the home and grounds for public tours, giving future generations a chance to glimpse a truly gilded era in our history.

To my knowledge, no one today lives in such lavish luxury in America. Nor does any American live in the dire poverty that existed in the same time frame either. We sometimes forget that we can be considered poor or well below the average income in America, and live far above the average in the majority of the rest of the world.

That's very evident in our struggle with illegal immigrant workers. We often fail to realize that while we tend to not want low-paying jobs, never mind minimum wages, people from less fortunate nations would love to have those jobs, and they deeply appreciate the opportunity to make what *they* consider to be good money.

We often struggle to help those who are struggling.

The impact of many political issues is not as immediately noticeable. Yet, the tug-of-war pulls back and forth.

Consider language. If I decide to live in France, I should not expect them to speak English or print signs in English for me. I should learn French. If I live in Spain, I should learn Spanish. If I live in Japan, I should learn Japanese. This is common sense.

Also true is the fact that I will be at a language disadvantage while I am learning French, or Spanish, or Japanese, or whatever language I need to learn. This is temporary. This is part of adjusting to a new culture. I would and should not expect that nation to adjust to me or the cultural comfortability that I bring with me.

Our history shows wave after wave of immigrants arriving on our shores. Each moved through the struggles of adjustment to their new world, including the new language… English.

Older generations, as is typical to our species, adapted more slowly or not at all. Children adapted quickly, except in families or neighborhoods that squelched their growth and assimilation. I call that a variation of the "Mother Hen Syndrome," where a family overprotects the offspring... with the best intentions, but not the best results for the young.

Where I was a child was a very large French-Canadian population, many of whom had parents, grandparents, and great-grandparents who had moved to the U.S.A. for the booming industries in our New England mill yards. Textiles, shoes, railroad engines, and much more came out of these highly productive mills.

Foreign workers stuck together, amidst typically horrific work conditions. They worked 14-18 hour days, 6 and 7 days a week. They earned miniscule money. Women also worked, earning far less and enduring far more. Even little children worked long hours in the mills, so schooling was often, unfortunately, sacrificed or very limited.

They endured. They were proudly forging a better life for the next generations.

Rivalries raged between immigrant groups. In my area, it was Greek versus French-Canadian. A river literally served as a dividing line of sorts.

Then came the next generation, benefitting from advancing labor laws and laws that protected children from labor abuses. Now children could go to school and learn English.

My classmates spoke English. Many had a grandparent living in their home. These grandparents often did not speak English. "Everything in time" is an expression that applies.

In recent years, I've sensed an unhealthy dose of what I call "Microwave Mentality." We have no patience. When we are not willing to change, we demand society change to meet our needs.

When the French moved to America, they learned English. So did the Spaniards, Irish, Scottish, and Dutch. So did Scandinavians, Belgians, Germans, and Italians. The same goes for Portuguese,

Israelis, and Armenians. Africans, even those brought here not by their own choice, learned English.

Each culture knew its oldest members might not adapt easily to the change, but they did their best. They sought a chance for a better life for their future generations.

They came here for opportunities, not guarantees.

Now we have 70+ languages in our schools. Are we helping or hindering by providing translators everywhere, rather than fully teaching English?

I think this speaks more about the dissolution of our family units than about language and culture. As young people in the past learned English, they helped their parents and grandparents.

Now we seem to have developed a concept that if I lose my native language, I lose my culture, my identity, my connection. I disagree.

On the other hand, I think that Americans are highly illiterate when it comes to languages. Europeans readily learn 5, 6, or 7 languages. We learn one… and we don't exactly speak English very well by anyone's standards.

When in groups in Europe, I was one embarrassed student as the others sought to communicate in a language that was not the native tongue for any of us. I could barely get by with Spanish, my only non-English option. I was truly the group dummy.

We've already touched on the issue of immigration. With all the world violence today, the issue gets fiery headlines. America has enjoyed being a diverse melting pot for generations. Still, something has clearly changed and not for the better.

Throngs of families, cultures, and individuals flocked here, primarily for economic opportunities or to escape political, religious, or ideological persecution. They came for the chance to build a better life. They did *not* come here for handouts or freebies.

I believe that remains true today.

Yet, somehow in the mix, we have a bitterness. There are groups of people determined to destroy us and our way of life. They don't offer a better alternative. They just hate. In particular, they hate freedom.

These haters aren't from one nation any longer. They are both young and old, male and female, black and white, educated and uncultured. They are within our borders in every state. They are outside our nation and throughout the world.

With such hate-filled people rushing to get established in many nations around the globe, we are in a very bad place. We cannot bomb Syria, Iran, Iraq or any other area and expect to obliterate the haters or the hatreds that have caused such unrest and violence for many centuries.

The haters have moved here and been cultivated here. They are here. There. Everywhere.

Unfortunately, they have mostly sprung out of one faith. Extremists from any ilk are dangerous. Period.

When they take advantage of our freedoms in order to advocate and teach destructive and criminal and inhuman paths of action, we all lose.

Most Americans do not fear someone because they happen to be Muslim. We fear people who hate us and who do not seem interested in considering tolerance. The majority of Muslims who try to immigrate here do so for a better life, not to destroy life.

We didn't fear all Christians when extremists bombed buildings or shot up people in health clinics. We recognized these murderous people were not typical. They were criminal.

But then arrived waves from a culture with which we are not familiar. Human nature took over. We distrust. We fear. Further complicating the scenario is the fact that some Muslim leaders in America choose to harbor and support extremists, even when they know they mean harm to our society.

No, I do not believe Muhammed would have approved. It is these vile, violent, hate-filled extremists that pose the danger. We can't just work to identify them and keep them out. They will wreak their havoc anywhere they can... anywhere around the globe.

They will find deranged, disturbed sympathizers everywhere. Unhappy, anger-filled people are highly susceptible to their message of destruction and terrorism.

Winning the war on terrorism will take generations in much the same way as we learn new languages or unlearn other hatreds, such as racism.

We need time. We need continuous positive examples and messages. We need peaceful compassion and humanity.

Tip: *"I hope our wisdom will grow with our power, and teach us, that the less we use our power the greater it will be."*
                                        -- Thomas Jefferson (1743 – 1826)
                                        3rd President of the United States

21
Rampant Racism and Divisiveness

"A free race cannot be born of slave mothers."
-- Margaret Sanger (1879 - 1966)
American educator, writer and nurse

One early autumn evening, Ron and I were visiting my husband's youngest daughter in Philadelphia. Ron's eldest son was with us as we walked up the hill to her lovely row home.

"Ah, there go some of our neighborhood white trash." Then laughter cackled from the trio of women lounging on the front stoop of their row home across the street.

Okay, this is a mostly black Philadelphia neighborhood. Still, I couldn't help but wonder what other drivel, both racist and other, these "ladies" were teaching to the next generation.

I chose to not be insulted. They were putting themselves down, suggesting that only white trash would be near their home. I felt sad for them in their ignorance. This was a nice neighborhood.

In Chapter 6 "Theories and Pseudo-Science" in **The Bimbo Has Brains**, I noted that, "Before we can stop applying foolish stereotypes to people, we will need to stop teaching them to the newest generation of children." Perhaps we all need such reminders of that fact from time to time.

Over the years, a great many people have worked hard to stop racism and help people have better lives. In fact, following a race riot in Springfield, Illinois, people recognized that help was needed to assist against the ignorance and violence being perpetrated against African Americans in the U.S.A. In 1909, as we mentioned earlier, a group of primarily white people organized a group focused on legal action and education. The N.A.A.C.P., or National Association for the Advancement of Colored People was born.

In the century-plus since, many improvements have been realized. Unfortunately, at the same time, many challenges have been endured. We humans are slow to change. Lots of people have worked hard to keep positive change advancing. Most of these efforts are at the grass roots level in cities and towns all across America. Other times we see very high-profile people calling for action.

Actors have often used their celebrity to bring attention to issues dear to them, but you don't expect to see them doing so in the middle of a Broadway play or a film. Usually, they choose an open, public forum, because people who bought a ticket to see one thing, typically are less than impressed to get something for which they did not choose to pay.

Occasionally, someone has used their moment in the spotlight to receive an award as a bully pulpit to protest something. Even people who expressed empathy with "the issue" typically criticize the poor choice of forum. Protesting in front of people there to see someone in a different capacity is akin to blindsiding them. It's picking the low hanging fruit. It's easy. We have a built-in audience for our "statement."

I must reiterate. I feel far more respect for celebrities who get actively involved in the issue instead. Use celebrity to call attention to the issue, sure, but prove your heart by personal involvement, no matter how uncelebrated it may be.

A good example is made by David Ortiz, the former Red Sox baseball player known as Big Papi. He has used his star power to help save hundreds of children in poverty in the Dominican Republic, his homeland. He didn't need to do it at the ballpark. He kept Fenway Park as his workplace. His heart's workplace, however, is the rest of the world.

His children's fund helps needy children in the United States, the Dominican Republic, and beyond. Big Papi uses various activities to raise awareness and money, from his own charity wine label to a sweepstakes to win a game of catch with the superstar.

Rampant Racism and Divisiveness

Many other celebrities, from athletes and authors to actors and musicians, have also become actively engaged in the causes nearest and dearest to their hearts. However, just as all of us, stars can tend to lose perspective sometimes. We all suffer lapses in judgement. We can all likely recall moments in our lives where we recognize that we could have done something better, used better timing, or chosen better words.

On August 27, 2016, the second-string NFL quarterback for the San Francisco 49ers, Colin Kaepernick, refused to stand for the National Anthem. Wearing socks that featured cartoon pigs wearing police hats, Kaepernick had said that the American flag stands for "a country that oppresses black people and people of color."

He had refused to stand during the anthem at all the first 3 of the 49ers' preseason games, but that Friday marked the first time he did so in uniform. That made all the difference. During the season opener, he sat in protest of police violence and black oppression, but he knelt in subsequent games, hoping to be less offensive to our military.

A lot of Americans have fought and died for his right to do so, but he could have made smarter choices, to say the least. Still, in 2017, Kaepernick's example was followed for a few weeks by players from virtually all the NFL teams. They wanted to show their outrage over racial oppression and police brutality against Blacks in America.

So, where is their outrage over Blacks shooting Blacks? The numbers show that this happens in Chicago to the amount of 12 per day. In my opinion, that is outrageous. Those numbers are egregiously higher than police violence against Blacks.

Oppression? We are far from perfect, but they should compare the United States with Muslim nations where, for example, women are forced to hide their faces and not leave their homes alone. And being gay is an automatic death sentence. Perhaps they should consider celebrating the freedoms and opportunities in the U.S.A.

These well-intended football players ended up alienating millions of people. This happened, not because their cause was unjust, but the forum was questioned. A black football player, making more money in one season than the vast majority of Americans will ever amass over the course of their entire lives, can be hard-pressed to be taken seriously protesting racial oppression.

If they want to use their celebrity to call attention to social issues, great, but they might have been more effective had they not chosen to use their professional sport event as the forum. Think about it.

Is it our best choice to do something disrespectful to show that we think someone else did something disrespectful?

After that first game, Colin Kaepernick had shared his reasons for the openly disrespectful act. I thought he had missed the point, though he was trying to make a point. Our flag. Our anthem. These were not the issues.

Incidents had occurred that made him and others want to protest police brutality. That's perfectly okay, even admirable. However, we don't have to disrespect fans, flag, and country to do that.

Kaepernick had reportedly signed a 6-year, $114-million contract with $60-million guaranteed, including a $12,328,766 signing bonus. That made his average annual salary a cool $19 million. This alone makes it easy to understand the public's disgust. This was no struggling quarterback. He was mostly trying to make a point for mankind… or perhaps make a name for himself.

Had he thought it through, he could have had a powerful impact using his wealth and celebrity for great good through social activism in the inner cities or to make positive changes in laws or law enforcement. In the end, Kaepernick chose to opt out of his contract rather than risk being released. Later, we heard him say that he would do anything to have another chance to play in the NFL. Hindsight does tend to be 20-20. Interesting perhaps, is the fact that Colin Kaepernick is biracial. He was adopted and raised by two white parents.

At the time when this started in August, 2016, many news commentators quickly reminded viewers of many things:

- Dr. Martin Luther King, Jr., would never disrespect the flag or another person to make a point.
- We do best to use our voice and influence to call for positive change, but not by negative actions.
- Kaepernick's act was a great disappointment to many people, especially American football fans.
- He had an exercised his right to freedom of expression.

My thought on that was simple. Thank God he lives in this oppressive U.S.A. that provides him with that right.

Learning that they were not rallying followers as much as annoying fans, some NFL players who had initially followed suit in the kneeling protest, then tried to appear more respectful by placing their hand on their heart when bowing their heads. No, it didn't look reverent. It looked out of place.

This was not the best forum. This teaches others, particularly youngsters, to make irreverent choices in any situation they want.

I started to wonder if we couldn't and shouldn't be treating the acts differently. Publicity and mass media coverage encourage any behavior. Here we had hundreds of thousands of people enjoying and respecting each game's opening ceremonies in the stadiums and millions watching on television on any given Sunday. Perhaps the media could proportionately focus on some of *them*, rather than zooming in on the protestors who were not protesting the NFL.

Not that it was in protest, but I recall streaking becoming a "hot mess" at baseball stadiums. At first, cameras tried to capture the action without being revealing of the nakedness. Then policy or practice changed, and media absolutely never put the camera on someone streaking naked across the field.

Media could choose to not focus on an out-of-place protest in the same manner. The kneeling protest had absolutely *nothing* to do with NFL rules, the stadium, the fans, or the game. So, in my opinion and that of millions of others, it was out of place.

That said, in 1968, two black American sprinters served up one of the most recognized demonstrations ever presented by athletes. Tommie Smith and John Carlos won gold and bronze medals in the Mexico City Olympics. With everyone on their feet, the first notes of the "Star-Spangled Banner" rang out. Both Americans carried through with their plan to make a statement by pushing a black-gloved fist into the air signaling Black Power.

What most people may not realize is that they also wore no shoes, just black socks, to protest black poverty in America. All three podium athletes wore buttons calling for human rights, but Australian silver medalist Peter Norman did not know the Americans would take the protest further.

The 1960's had been a particularly tumultuous time in America, with protests raging from anti-war to racism and women's rights. Smith and Carlos initially said they were protesting for Blacks, but decades later they modified their reasoning to say the protest was not just for Blacks, but for all oppressed people everywhere.

They raised awareness and raised eyebrows, turning their 15 minutes of fame into a lifetime of controversy.

Nowadays, public sentiment has softened. In fact, their silent demonstration is seen more as a courageous act at a time when prejudice against Blacks was still rampant in the USA. Though we recognize their courage, particularly based on the social climate in the 1960's, it's a little tougher when it comes from multi-millionaires in 2017.

We just don't expect... or always understand... when someone protests something in a setting that has nothing to do with their purported social issue.

Think about it. You're in a movie theatre. Just after the climax of the film, one of the actresses turns to the camera and gives her verbal protest of something she perceives as a social injustice. And they released the film without editing it out.

Or you've invited a chef to do a demonstration preparing one of their recipes. After adding a few ingredients to the pan, they deviate into a diatribe on why they must leave their job and the nasty boss to start their own restaurant.

Perhaps you are at a concert, and the artist stops to viciously criticize the venue for not wishing to pay them extra money when they decided to add additional musicians at the last minute.

Or you are attending a live theatre production, and one of the actors suddenly turns to the audience and starts chanting some slogan to show support for a worthy cause near and dear to him.

A spin on that actually happened on Broadway just days after the 2016 Presidential election. At least they waited until the curtain call. The actor portraying Aaron Burr took the moment to "speak for everyone" and address the newly elected Vice-President Pence, who'd brought his family to that performance of "Hamilton."

Noting the cast's diversity in sex, race, creed and orientation, actor Brandon Victor Dixon said, "We are the diverse America who are alarmed and anxious that your new administration will not protect us, our planet, our children, our parents, or defend us and uphold our inalienable rights, sir. But we truly hope this show has inspired you to uphold *our* American values and work on behalf of *all* of us. *All* of us." Dixon gestured broadly to the cast beside and behind him.

Was the cast responding to an actual threat by the incoming Trump-Pence administration, or were they alarmed by a *perceived* threat concocted by the media and Democrat Party opponents to Republicans in general and Donald Trump in particular? Naturally, with constant repetition, the perceived threat had become "reality" for many people, although no facts backed it up. In the end, will this one day be seen as courageous… Or will it be forgotten as opportunistic or out-of-place? That is not for any of us to judge.

Such action makes me ponder. Perhaps I wear rose-colored glasses, but what makes us, as people, think that *any*one elected to our nation's highest offices has no intention of representing everyone, following the law, or doing a good job? Further, what makes us think that even the best of any President's planned good deeds can get through the murky mires of Washington politics intact?

Regardless, I ask people to please pick a forum on their own time, not when I've paid money to be at an event that was *not* meant for their particular political statement, regardless of how vital or popular they may believe it is.

I agree with the theatre-goers who expressed disappointment. I would have been annoyed also… at best. On the other hand, I also agree with the theatre-goers who expressed pleasure. This is a free country, and we enjoy an unusual right to free speech, even if it annoys others.

What gets my ire is a tonality and behavior that says, "I'm okay; you are *not*." That translates to mean that I think *my* opinions and beliefs are valuable, but *yours* are misguided. That's just not healthy. If I express my belief, and it differs from my friend's belief, I do not expect it to affect our friendship. If it does, then I am not the one with "issues."

All opinions and thoughts should be valued, NOT just when we are in agreement.

However, when I think someone is being bullied, I support the person coming under attack! I can't help it. I have always felt akin to those being bullied, whether on a playground or from any bully pulpit of their choosing.

Would you be AOK if you're at your child's birthday party with many of your friends and neighbors in your backyard celebrating, and suddenly one of them unfurls a huge banner espousing their favorite cause?

Or, would you be okay if you're at your (or a family member's) college graduation and, as the graduates enter the stadium, two of them halt the processional and raise their fists in the air in a protest of some important cause?

Here's my deal. The causes may all be very worthy. They all may warrant attention. But is doing something to grab attention away from the focus of that event fair to others? Those protesting rarely think about others.

Why treat people unfairly because you think someone else has been treated unfairly? Or you think they might be about to be treated unfairly. That's illogical.

Such protests may well be an easy way to get people talking about an issue. However, it may also be unfair and disrespectful, at the very least, to everyone else who has the right to NOT have their celebration or ceremony or event interrupted or slammed with a forced distraction.

Consider the following, despite the dramatic horror. People are at a wedding or at a church. Some, who disagree with their faith and don't want to see it practiced, choose to disrupt the proceedings. They fire shots. They explode a bomb. Innocent people lie dead. Celebration turns to insane chaos.

The attackers got attention by their misdeeds, but the only supporters they are apt to attract are those who are off-kilter in their shared thinking.

If we believe that terrorizing and killing innocent people in the name of our cause is acceptable, then we do not believe in Life, Liberty, and the Pursuit of Happiness.

Black Lives Matter. Hello! **All** lives matter. Period. Lies Matter, too, so we need to focus on not letting our politicians or other leaders tell them, especially not repeatedly.

By the way, black racism against Whites does not justify white racism against Blacks any more than white racism against Blacks justifies black racism against Whites. Racial hatred is wrong. Period.

All hate is wrong. Period.

I believe my support solidified for Donald Trump when so many of those protesting revealed themselves to be opposite what I believe is right. I "get it" that many young people were afraid. Their fears had been regularly fed by mainstream media, privileged academics, and celebrity elitists.

Fear often haunts those on the losing side of a Presidential election.

However, bullies, torture, tormenting, shooting, demeaning, and more should never be tolerated. This especially contradicts the genuine feelings that had been expressed... peacefully... by those who had been taught to be fearful of a Donald Trump America.

News accounts of true expressions of hatred and viciousness are far too frequent, from both sides. This fact needs addressing. This we should not ever tolerate.

You may recall a January, 2016 event where four black young adults kidnapped, ridiculed, and tortured their white, mentally challenged "friend" for being a Donald Trump supporter. Laughing throughout their insidiousness, they shared their crimes "live" via social media. They thought this was funny. They thought wrong.

Remember the young white male who walked into a black church in Charleston, South Carolina in June, 2015. He let the group pray for and with him. Then he drew his gun and shot them, killing 9 innocent people. He defended himself at his trial, and he expressed no regret, only continued hatred and racism. He thought the jury 1should not give him the death penalty, contending that there were *reasons* for his hatred. He thought wrong.

Early in the Presidential Primary season, in October, 2015, a black man in Atlanta, Georgia, was recorded by onlookers as he denounced President Barack Obama and announced his support for Donald Trump. He explained to people, "Obama has failed us. We are taking back America. I voted for him twice, and he broke my heart." This man explained why black people should be supporting Donald Trump. He even said that he'd stand alone for Donald Trump. A voice in the crowd called out, assuring him that he'd not be standing alone.

I met Alfonso, a remarkable cab driver. He'd only been 15 years old when political hell broke loose in his homeland of Jamaica in 1976. He survived the heinous violence that accompanied the democratic socialist party rule under Prime Minister Michael Manley.

Interestingly, I had visited a college classmate there in 1976 and saw first-hand how terribly the nation struggled. Lawlessness pervaded the nation, fires burned in the cities, radio jingles insisted people re-elect Manley, and the government started confiscating passports of its business people and taking over private businesses. When the opposition leader, Edward Seaga, finally took over in 1980, the damage had already been done, despite desperate public relation campaigns to try to get tourists to "come back to Jamaica."

As of November, 2017, Alphonso had been in the U.S.A. for 26 years and is very proud of becoming a citizen. A black conservative, he endures great criticism. He says that we don't understand what is happening to our nation. No way does he want socialism or even left-leaning leaders. He saw how it destroyed his country. Alphonso warns that we take our freedoms for granted. That is why he says he always votes Republican, as he says, "For the people. For the workers. For the nation."

Of course, there is the other side. In Boston, Massachusetts, two men were arrested for urinating on a homeless man. They claimed to have been "inspired by Donald Trump." Quack, quack.

In Hollywood, a homeless black woman tried to protect Trump's Star on the Walk of Fame, a star he'd been honored with in 2007. Aggravated Democrats laughed at her. Hillary Clinton supporters openly attacked her with vicious name calling, as the woman repeatedly expressed that she supported Donald Trump. These haters tore up her signs, pushed her down, and admonished others on the street to *not* to call for help for her. They smashed the Star.

Disagreeing with *them* made *you* "hate-filled," even though, in truth, *they* were the ones spewing hateful and racist comments… behaving violently toward people for daring to believe differently. We need some mirror searching here. Duh.

Nothing happened to these nasty folks. Donald Trump's star was simply replaced later.

In July, 2016, a black Trump supporter called out a reporter for race-baiting. He noted that it didn't matter if white supremacists support Trump, because Trump is not a racist. The man was tired of constant media attempts to associate Donald Trump with racism. The media had given people those perceptions, and voters were getting sick of it.

Video showed a black Trump supporter imploring a MSNBC host to "stop with all the racist stuff. We're all Americans." The black man showed class. The MSNBC host? Not so much.

In September, 2016, "Trump and Republicans Are Not Racist" T-shirts were worn by a group of black men as they spoke out, calling for all people of all races to open their eyes and stop believing Hollywood, the media, and traditional hype from other Democrats.

Oh, and here's a way to not influence someone to vote the way you prefer. A black military veteran was shot in the leg for admitting he was going to vote for Donald Trump. There are just so many things wrong with that scenario that I don't know where to begin.

Back in February, 2016, Pastor Mark Burns, who happens to be black, announced that he would not be lining up with the majority of Blacks to support Hillary Clinton or Bernie Sanders. He eloquently noted that Hillary Clinton had spent decades being the very racist and bigot she repeatedly accused Donald Trump of being. He begged people not to listen to the lies and rhetoric. Burns went on to explain that Hillary and Democrats had long-championed abortion of black babies as a way to exterminate Blacks. He shared statistics showing blacks to comprise 13% of the population, with black women having 40% of the abortions.

It is true that in 1921 Margaret Sanger formed the American Birth Control League, which became Planned Parenthood, along with creating the Negro Project to decrease black populations. People don't like hearing such facts, but that's just part of actuality.

Race, sex, religion, whatever.... It's at least grotesquely misguided and unproductive to hate someone who is different. I don't have to be judgmental to know the difference between basic right and wrong.

> *"The world is too dangerous for anything but truth*
> *and too small for anything but love."*
> -- William Sloane Coffin (1924 – 2006)
> American Clergyman and Peace Activist

I remember hearing plenty of discussions during President Barack Obama's eight years in the White House about how racism seemed to be getting encouraged and supported. This seemed opposite of what one might have expected would happen with a person with African heritage finally serving as President.

When he'd first been elected in 2008, Michelle Obama garnered criticism for stating, "For the first time in my adult life, I am proud of my country." Classy as she is, First Lady Laura Bush defended Michelle Obama, suggesting that she'd probably meant "more proud," not that she'd *never* been proud at all. Unfortunately, Michelle Obama didn't seem to learn the "comradery" aspect of First Ladies, as she was getting her digs in on Melania Trump following the 2016 election.

Hillary Clinton supporters joined the battle cries, calling both black and white Trump supporters by various derogatory names, including ignorant, stupid, idiots, faggots, racists, and bigots. And yet, it was on November 5, 2016, just before the election, that Hillary Clinton herself said, "I am sick and tired of the negative, dark, divisive, dangerous vision and behavior of people who support Donald Trump."

She was missing the fact that it was the negative, dark, divisive, dangerous vision and behavior of people who supported Hillary Clinton of which she seemed to be speaking. She was entitling herself to her own facts, and she was not going to let the truth stand in the way of them.

I guess she hoped everyone would forget that just a few weeks earlier she had inspired a great many people to vote *for* Donald Trump, when she'd thought it witty to quip that she could put "half of Trump's supporters in what I call the basket of Deplorables." She elaborated, calling them racist, sexist, homophobic, xenophobic, and Islamophobic.

Millions of Americans, black and white, male and female, gay and straight, natural born and immigrant, immediately started proudly calling themselves part of "The Deplorables."

Clinton rightly observed that we were in a "volatile political environment." Unfortunately, she chose to add fuel to that fire.

This whole race came as a surprise to her. She'd seemingly found it laughable to think that Donald Trump could ever be taken seriously or be elected President of the United States. She certainly never thought he could honestly win against her. She continued to paint a negative picture of Donald Trump, which drew more supporters to him, rather than to her. Boomerang Bullying.

Democratic agitators warned that Trump supporters would not accept the election results when he lost. They told people nationwide to prepare for violence and protests by rabid, racist Trump supporters.

Hmmm… after the election we saw protests… violence, destruction of public property, putrid spewing of hatred, refusals to accept the newly elected President. However, the protests came *not* from violent, angry, Donald Trump supporters, but from violent, angry Hillary Clinton supporters.

Destroying personal and public property was somehow "okay" for them, because they felt their cause was justified. Hmmm… These activities are not protected under our right to peaceful protest.

On November 10, 2016, in Chicago, a black mob violently beat a white man because he had voted for Donald Trump. By-standers laughed. One person commented that the white guy deserved to be beaten because Whites had been enslaving and killing Blacks for so long. Hellooo!!!

Henry Davis, an outspoken black man from St. Louis, Missouri, took to social media after Trump's election to laugh at everyone who'd laughed at him for supporting Donald Trump. He also responded to the protestors following the inauguration of President Donald Trump, asking people what good Obama had done for America? He answered his own question with, "Nothing."

Also in St. Louis, some Black Lives Matter protestors went berserk, attacking a black Trump supporter for wearing his "Make America Great Again" cap. He responded with the logic that he wants jobs, not welfare. He said that he doesn't want to be a slave again. The protestors screamed at him. They had less than zero interest in hearing a different point of view, even from a black man who simply saw our burgeoning socialism and welfare system as enslaving people, particularly in his black community.

A couple of people made videos threatening to kill President Trump... and even members of his family. This, my friend, is the opposite of progressive. This is not protected under our right to free speech. This is domestic terrorism.

Be the change you want to see.
Hateful violence because people
believe or vote differently is not okay.
Period.

Reverend Martin Luther King, Jr. wanted a color-blind society. He did not advocate for one that treated Blacks as inferior and thus needing special programs and benefits.

As long as we humor, support, or find racially separatist programs relevant, we are clinging to the divisiveness of racism, *and* we are overtly supporting reverse racism. Far worse, we are holding minorities down, insinuating that Blacks are inferior and need special assistance or exclusivity to compete. Intelligence dictates to all of us that this is totally false.

It confounds me that we not only accept, but we encourage exclusively "black" organizations, clubs, activities, awards, etc., while "white" counterparts would be not only frowned upon, but they would be forbidden. *That* is where we get and stay "squirrelly."

Rampant Racism and Divisiveness

Decades ago, Blacks needed to group together to feel strength to assert themselves in a formidably "white" society. But if we want Martin Luther King, Jr.'s colorblind society to ever be a reality, we have to stop all this social permitting, pandering, and prohibiting. It holds Blacks back now, and it just annoys non-Blacks as well as many Blacks.

These programs divide, not unify. They squelch, not uplift. Why have Black Music Awards, Miss Black America, or the National Black Deaf Advocates? Can you imagine if someone tried to hold a White Music Awards or a Miss White America Pageant? And are hearing and deafness advocacy efforts for everyone somehow leaving out Blacks?

There also seem to be more than 100 black colleges & universities in the USA. Are there any white colleges?

I saw an article by Ben Taylor, formerly of Graphiq, revealing the "10 Least Diverse Colleges in America." Predominantly white colleges were highlighted since a few had 85% white students. A correction was later issued, since it should have listed them perhaps as the whitest colleges in America. When it comes to the "least diverse," they'd had a number of readers point out that some US colleges have 90% black or Hispanic students, lacking diversity far more than the "worst offending," so-called "too white" colleges.

Of course, we can look at Edinboro, Pennsylvania. The city's crime rate is 25 times lower than the average American city. It is among the safest and whitest places to live. Edinboro University of Pennsylvania is located in the city of Edinboro, where the study found 88% Caucasian students. Interestingly, the city also has 88% Caucasian residents.

South Dakota State University is one of 31 colleges and universities in the state of South Dakota. Typical of a South Dakotan school, it is 91% white. Ummm… less than 2% of South Dakota's population is Black. This means their schools host a larger % of black students than even exist in the state's population.

The Bimbo Has *MORE* Brains

I worked for James Reynolds, a wonderful man who was the Dean of Admissions and Financial Aid at what's now called Southern New Hampshire University. He regularly testified in Washington regarding higher education financial aid issues.

The problem was relatively simple. His was not the only school of higher learning in the state. However, to meet the numbers needed to qualify for federal financial aid, some brilliant politicos would require his school to enroll every single black man, woman, and child in New Hampshire.

Obviously, that was impossible. Even if his team could get the needed numbers, what about all the other colleges and universities in the State? Who on earth would think it is logical to force colleges to enroll more people from minorities than even live in the entire state?

The bottom line is that we don't want schools discriminating against Blacks or Whites or any other group. Often numbers that appear warped simply reflect student interest. For example, coming in #1 on the list of the least diverse colleges was Beth Medrash Govoha. Dedicated to the study of Jewish religious texts, this school is "the whitest" in America with a 97% white student body. Thankfully, the study acknowledged that the school is not discriminating, since almost all the applicants are also white.

I find it interesting, if not downright disturbing that colleges are criticized for being "too white." There were two colleges in the 90 percentile of students being non-black. However, other colleges were celebrated for having high percentages of black students, despite few or no white students. Somehow *that* is okay.

Several credible sources publish "Top 10," "Top 15," "Top 30," and "Top 50" lists of the best "historically black colleges and universities." Imagine publishing such lists of the best "historically white colleges and universities." You can find these lists from Time Magazine, US News & World Report, and numerous websites like CollegeChoice.com, BestColleges.com, Niche.com, and InfoPlease.com, to name a few.

Rampant Racism and Divisiveness

I recognize that following the Civil War, all-black schools made it possible for African-American citizens to get higher educations in a still highly-prejudiced society. Today, however, I find celebrations of such to be highly divisive, at best.

We are not looking at 1 or 2 institutions boasting black, non-Hispanic student populations of over 90%. The 2017 numbers from the College Press reveal more than a dozen schools with more than 90% black students, and more than 30 with at least 75% black, non-Hispanic students.

Check it out yourself. Lane College in Jackson, Tennessee, for example, had 100% black students. Morris College 97%, Saint Augustine's University 96%, and Morehouse College, Virginia Union University, Central State University (Ohio), and South Carolina State University all at 95%. Martin University 94% and both Florida Agricultural & Mechanical University and Southern University at New Orleans at 93%.

That does *not* reflect a desire to evolve into Martin Luther King, Jr.'s vision of a colorblind America. He didn't seek special circumstances. He encouraged fellow black Americans to excel on the same playing fields with the same opportunities.

Personally, I don't care if there are predominantly black universities, as long as folks stop criticizing schools that happen to be predominantly white. None of us should expect to have it both ways.

Tip:
"I have decided to stick with love. Hate is too great a burden to bear."
--Rev. Martin Luther King, Jr. (1929 – 1968)
American Baptist Minister and Civil Rights Activist

22
Bimbo Bits

"Be more concerned with your character than with your reputation.
Your character is what you really are,
while your reputation is merely what others think you are."
— Dale Carnegie (1888 – 1955)
American Writer and Lecturer

We'll look at a wide variety of our human facets now. One of the most important of these, especially when we are trying to survive and thrive in challenging times, is a great sense of humor.

Since 1985, comedian Steven Wright, noted for his deadpan comic style, has toyed with our minds through his humor. He says things like, "Why is it a penny for your thoughts, but you have to put your two cents in? Somebody's making a penny."

One of my personal favorites is, "I went to a place to eat. It said, 'breakfast at any time.' So, I ordered French Toast during the Renaissance."

The list goes on and on. "I have a microwave fireplace. I like it. I can lay down for an evening in front of the fire in 8 minutes."

"I got stopped once for speeding, and the officer said, 'Don't you know the speed limit is 55 miles an hour?' I said, 'Yes, I do, but I wasn't going to be out that long.'"

"You can't have everything. Where would you put it?"

And one of his classics: "I spilled spot remover on my dog, and now he's gone."

A brilliantly well-spoken friend of mine, the best-selling author Richard Lederer, captures our imaginations and sensibilities through his unique combination of rapid-fire wit and firm grasp on the obvious... and perhaps the oblivious.

Bimbo Bits

His books, including 1987's **Anguished English**, make me laugh repeatedly. Most of us are familiar with Lederer's puns and other linguistic observations:

- "Why do we drive on a parkway and park in a driveway?"
- "Why does night fall, but day breaks?"
- "What's a skeleton's favorite food? Spare ribs."
- "How can the words 'raise' and 'raze' sound the same, but mean the opposite?"
- "Why are a wise man and a wise guy opposites?"

Even as kids we had humorous books playing with oxymorons like "jumbo shrimp." Or "larger half." Consider my favorite: "unbiased opinion."

We are very strange beasts, we humans. However, I think we are healthier people when we learn to laugh at ourselves.

In the early 1990's I recall the old, running gag on "The Arsenio Hall Show" where he'd ponder "things that make us go Hmmm." These could have come straight out of some of Lederer's many books or even Wright's comic sketches. They remain timeless and have inspired many similar "lines."

As you have observed in this book, "hmmm" is part of my regular conversation. We all have thoughts and experiences that inspire such a response.

Hmmm

While driving, we often see yellow highway signs: deer crossing, moose crossing, panther crossing... next 2, 4, 9, or whatever number of miles. How *do* these animals know to cross the highways in these zones? Hmmm.

I believe there's a law in this country that requires our lawmakers to live under the same regulations they pass for us. Hmmm.

My husband was talking with me about my writing career. He quipped, "That's not work. You enjoy it!" Hmmm. Newsflash. It's okay to love your work. Enjoying what we do doesn't make it "not work." It simply makes our work more enjoyable.

Some women are born leaders. Some leaders are born women. Hmmm.

We can also consider everyday scenarios and arguments that seem to have no solutions. A guy leaves the toilet seat up. The gal wants it left down. Well, we could solve this battle by agreeing to prevent bacteria splashing into the bathroom.

We do this by lowering the toilet seat cover <u>before</u> flushing. Thus, before using the toilet, everyone lifts… either the cover or the seat and the cover. Before flushing, everyone lowers… either the cover or the seat & cover. If this can't be handled, is it not both lazy *and* unhealthy? Hmmm.

While on the subject, should the toilet paper roll from over or under the roll? Toilet paper manufacturers settled this quandary years ago, when they came out with printed papers. To see the prints, consumers had to load the toilet paper so it rolls from over the top. You can still load it any which way you want, but manufacturers say that over the top rules the rolls. Hmmm.

If time heals all wounds, how come bellybuttons don't fill in? Hmmm.

In court, why do they ask if you swear to tell the truth? If you're planning on lying, do they really think you'll tell them so? Hmmm.

If you try to fail, and succeed, which have you done? Hmmm.

> *"Campaign behavior for wives: Always be on time.*
> *Do as little talking as humanly possible.*
> *Lean back in the parade car so everybody can see the president."*
> -- Eleanor Roosevelt (1884 – 1962)
> First Lady to 32nd President of the United States

Bimbo Bits

"When people ask me why I am running as a woman,
I always answer, 'What choice do I have?'"
-- Pat Schroeder (1940 -)
First Woman to represent Colorado in U.S. House of
Representatives

T-Shirt Messages
It seems silly sometimes, but words of wisdom and silliness can be found in some interesting places. I call these the T-shirt messages.

INEPTOCRACY - "A system of government where the least capable to lead are elected by the least capable to produce, and where members of society least likely to sustain themselves or succeed are rewarded with goods and services paid for by the confiscated wealth of a diminishing number of producers."

Those are some sad, but often true words I read on a T-shirt. I guess recognizing it as both sad and funny, and yet true, guarantees my place on the list of politically incorrect people. That's just fine with me. I do not ever want to be dubbed as politically correct. I'd rather be honest and factual.

We see lots of thematic or funny quips on T-shirts.
- Faith Over Fear
- I speak my mind because it hurts to bite my tongue
- You can't drink all day if you don't start in the morning
- I speak fluent sarcasm
- Don't grow up... It's a trap!

One great shirt walked past us at a local steakhouse restaurant. Inspiring our spontaneous chuckles, it simply read,
"I eat Vegans."

Or consider this gem.
If we lie to government, it's a felony.
If government lies to us, it's politics.

The Bimbo Has *MORE* Brains

A Bee in My Bonnet

"Too bad that all the people who really know how to run the country are busy driving taxi cabs and cutting hair."
-- George Burns (1896 – 1996)
American Comedian, Actor, and Singer

My husband gets openly annoyed with me when we get talking politics, because I am so sickened by it all in recent years. Here are a few things that stir up a "bee in my bonnet," so to speak.

I think it's shameful that increasing property taxes drive retirees and elderly people out of their homes. The government doesn't care that you're now on a fixed income in a retirement that you earned after years of hard work and hearty support of the community.

I think it's nearly criminal that our military veterans return home after serving and sacrificing and don't get solid support and medical care for the rest of their lives.

I think it's divisive that we continue to propagate and propel racial differences, breeding hatred and distrust, helping only select groups, rather than celebrating our similarities and promoting American opportunities for all.

I think it's un-American that some people think it's justifiable to try to squelch someone *else's* right to free speech by screaming, yelling, and being disruptive under the guise of *their* "right to free speech." The political process is disgusting enough without sinking to its level.

I'm sick and tired of so many people not working when they are every bit as capable as the next person. These are people who won't work. I have no interest in paying their way, nor should I be taxed to support laziness. The vicious cycle it creates in each subsequent generation is way out of control.

Then, to add insult to injury, some people complain that they don't *want* to take the available jobs for unskilled workers, because then they wouldn't be able to afford their lifestyle. Sooo, people who *do* work should have less ability to enjoy the lifestyle they've earned, so that those who won't work can live better?!? That is very warped thinking.

That doesn't mean the minimum wage is too low, by the way. It means the person's work ethic is too low, *and* the "hand out" lifestyle is too high. Workers (a.k.a. Taxpayers) should not be footing the bill to allow people who *refuse* to work to live at a higher lifestyle level than those who *do* work.

Duh! If people lack work ethic to begin with, why cripple them with a lifestyle they refuse to earn… or even understand that they *should* actually earn… themselves. If they won't go to work because they'd suffer a "cut in pay," then we're giving them way too much.

We need to help people build their self-esteem, confidence, and pride by having them work and earn at least some of their own way. Let's help them have some dignity, for crying out loud.

This is not the same as helping people who actually *need* help. I think we should all be willing to help someone who truly *can't* work… That's a hand up, not a hand out.

Okay, I'll get off my soap box now.

Which is more terrifying?
The possibility of Life on other planets… perhaps on hundreds of thousands of other planets… orrr… the possibility that in all the vastness of the universe, Earth is the *only* planet supporting Life… never mind Life as we know it?

Donald Trump as President of the United States… orrr… a U.S.A. that does not support peaceful transition of power and governance by someone not of our personal liking who happened to win the election?

Putting up with people we do not like... orrr... a society that supports violence against people we do not like?

People voting for someone you do not want to see win... orrr... people not caring enough to vote?

> *"I have yet to hear a man ask for advice on how to combine marriage and a career."*
> -- Gloria Steinem (1934 -)
> American Feminist and Political Activist

Priorities
> *"Nobody's life is ever all balanced. It's a conscious decision to choose your priorities every day."*
> -- Elizabeth Hasselbeck (1977 -)
> American Television Personality

In the movie, "Ocean's 11," George Clooney's character, Danny Ocean, comments on his ex-wife's new man. "Does he make you laugh?" Julie Roberts' character, Tess, quickly replies, "He doesn't make me cry."

In 2003, the Deputy Undersecretary of Defense in George H.W. Bush's administration was talking about France not joining the coalition forces to invade Iraq. Jed Babbin's comment answered the question, but not without an obvious show of sarcasm when he said, "Going to war without France is like going hunting without an accordion."

> *"What may be done at any time, will be done at no time."*
> -- Scottish Proverb

Partisan Humor

Our sense of humor seems quite slanted, depending on our point of view. This makes sense. We see value in our own philosophy and opinions... or we would change them.

For example, "What do you call a basement full of Liberals? A whine cellar."

In reality, both political parties tend to whine... a lot, especially when trying to point fingers at the other party. So, I think the joke should read, "What do you call a basement full of politicians? A whine cellar."

Here's another example. "What's the difference between God and a Conservative? God knows He's not a Republican."

I've listened to enough full-of-it politicos from both sides of the aisle to sense that most of them believe they deserve to be held in higher esteem than "regular folks." Thus, such a joke could just as easily read, "What's the difference between God and a Liberal? God knows He's not a Democrat."

Of course, some jokes are already equal opportunity insulters.

What do politicians and porn stars have in common? They are experts in switching positions in front of a camera.

What do you call a politician with an IQ of 130? A foursome.

What's the difference between a car and a politician? You get to test-drive a car.

P.O.L.I.T.I.C.S. = Purely Outright Lies Intended To Infect Common Sense

What do you call an honest man in the Oval Office? Lost.

Many of us lack a sense of humor when it comes to politics on any level. If we take issues seriously, we struggle to see humor, even if aimed at "the other guy." Or we feel very insulted by the suggestion that our political affiliation is stupid, ill-informed, or in any other way jaded.

So, when a joke casts "our side" in a negative light, we are not impressed. Consider this. How many Democrats does it take to clean up a disastrous Bush presidency? At least two!

Then, of course, there's the other side. How many Republicans does it take to clean up a disastrous Obama presidency? Just one... ANY one. The humor from both sides can only be called pathos.

Typically, comedians and jokes tend to be dramatically slanted to please either Liberals or Conservatives. Actually, I should note that they more often than not tilt toward the Left. Yup, it's rather common knowledge that media, entertainment, and arts, in general, lean left.

A good number seem to make a living off slamming anyone who even thinks moderately, never mind conservatively. I heard a humorist, Andy Kindler, picking some low-hanging fruit by jumping on the Republican National Convention bandwagon.

"Republicans are just rich, old, white people. That's all they are. Did you ever see the Republican National Convention? All white people. And six black people... paid actors. James Earl Jones in his most difficult, most challenging role! Tune in and watch him trying to look pleased during a George Bush speech." Seriously. This is very tired, old Democrat stuff.

Most liberal comedians are far more aware of the increasing numbers of economically struggling, young, and highly diverse Republicans. Despite numerous attempts to say otherwise, being hard-working, blue-collar, gay, female, or well-educated qualifies people to rightfully believe in the politics and policies of either party. There's more than one right way to get things done.

That said, let's continue to tick off one side.

Bimbo Bits

If February is Black History Month and March is Women's History Month, what are Republicans celebrating the rest of the year? Discrimination.

How is Donald Trump going to shut down the Department of Education? By renaming it Trump University.

What do you get when you offer a member of the Tea Party a penny for his thoughts? Change.

How does a Democrat get shot in Texas? He drives around in a car with a bumper sticker saying, "I voted for Obama, I'm gay, and I'm here to take your guns."

Naturally, there are plenty of jokes to reflect a different slant. So, now it's time to tick off the other side.

How do Democrats keep their breath fresh? With lots of Entitle-mints, of course.

What's worse than President Bill Clinton calling you a womanizer? Anthony Weiner or Eliot Spitzer calling you a pervert!

What's the difference between Elvis and a smart Liberal? People think they've actually seen Elvis.

In what way are Democrats more generous than Republicans? Unlike Republicans, Democrats are not only generous with their own money, but also with other people's money.

How can we know that Democrats are more diverse people? Because Democrats keep count of how many people they know in each racial or ethnic category.

Often, jabbing, yet insightful political comments come from folks who don't even live in the U.S.A. British political commentator, John Oliver, was speaking about Rod Blagojevich, the 40th governor of Illinois. He noted, "Four out of the last eight governors of Illinois have ended up in jail. That's 50%. If you grow up in South Central

L.A., you are said to have a 1-in-3 chance of ending up in prison. That's less than if you become governor of Illinois."

We tend to see the humor in political jabs due to the existence of at least a grain of truth. All too frequently, there's a grain *sack* full of truth.

We can easily pick on all politics from both sides of the aisle. There is certainly a plethora of jokes that tell both sides of every slanted story, with very little change in wording.

What do you call the idiots who spend their days mortified of aliens, Muslims, and gays? Fox News fans.
What do you call the idiots who spend their days mortified of police brutality, facts, and the Second Amendment? CNN Viewers.

What do you call a person who's confused about work ethic, economics, and family values? A Liberal.
What do you call a person who's confused about entitlements, racism, and global warming? A Conservative.

Okay, let's simplify this. In truth, we rarely need to change even a few words. We can literally replace Liberal with Conservative or Democrat with Republican in most of the political jabs out there. Each side howls gleefully along with their own side and looks down their noses at the other, pitying them for being so misguided.

Why are jokes about Liberals/Conservatives getting dumber and dumber? Because Democrats/Republicans have started to make them up themselves.

Why do most Liberals/Conservatives fail geometry? Because they don't have any points.

How do you confuse a Liberal/Conservative? You don't. They're born that way.

What is the definition of gross ignorance?
144 Democrats/Republicans.

How many Republicans / Democrats does it take to change a light bulb?

A) Three. One to change the bulb, one to alert the media to publicize it, and one to blame the electric bill on the other side of the aisle.

B) Just one, but it really gets screwed.

C) It's irrelevant; they still don't know they're in the dark!

D) All of the above.

A Conservative/Liberal found a genie's magic lamp and rubbed it. The genie emerged and said, "I will grant you one wish." The Conservative/Liberal said, "I wish I were smarter." So, the genie made him a Liberal/Conservative.

Now, here's a creepy one that reflects dark-comedy, a seedy side of human nature that we've seen emerge far too frequently.

A Republican/Democrat died, and a friend went around collecting for a fund for his funeral. Asked to donate ten dollars, a woman replied, "Ten dollars? It only takes ten dollars to bury a Republican/a Democrat? Here's a hundred; go bury ten of them!"

Tip: The man who can befriend someone who does not like him, is either a politician, and thus cannot be trusted, or a fool, and thus should not be a politician.

23
Everyone's a Critic

As I've mentioned earlier, in a time far away, I worked as an arts and entertainment reporter for a local television station. Regularly, I did critiques on plays, concerts, and various other festivals and fairs.

Today, everyone is a critic. We judge. We score. We rate everything. We offer thumbs up or thumbs down. We review places we visit and restaurants at which we dine. We complain. We make recommendations. We criticize.

We especially enjoy this great American past-time with regard to our politicians, especially our Presidents. While mainstream media attention and social media pervasiveness make our society's voices seem so much louder, not much has changed over the decades.

I am not saying the criticisms are or aren't warranted. I'm not saying whether they're accurate or off target, but they've been lobbed at our leaders since the U.S.A. was born.

Most of us think we are pretty savvy at knowing what Presidents were criticized and for what. Next are some actual criticisms that were flung at actual Presidents. How many can you guess right? (The correct answers will be at the chapter's end.) Here we go.

He escalated a war we shouldn't have been in at all.
> John F. Kennedy
> Lyndon B. Johnson
> George W. Bush
> Barack Obama

He's slow on civil rights at best and a racist at worst.
> John F. Kennedy
> Lyndon B. Johnson
> Ronald Reagan
> Barack Obama
> Donald Trump

He's a playboy at best and the worst womanizer ever.
> John F. Kennedy
> Lyndon B. Johnson
> Bill Clinton
> Donald Trump

He has no integrity.
> George Washington
> Warren Harding
> Richard Nixon

He has poor military knowledge.
> George Washington
> George W. Bush
> Barack Obama

He's too aristocratic/monarchial, megalo-maniacal.
> George Washington
> Ronald Reagan
> Donald Trump

He stole the Presidential election.
> John F. Kennedy
> George W. Bush
> Donald Trump

He's way too much of a cowboy to be President.
> Teddy Roosevelt
> Ronald Reagan
> George H. W. Bush

He's inept. The military will never take him seriously.
> Jimmy Carter
> Ronald Reagan
> George W. Bush
> Barack Obama
> Donald Trump

He's just a B-list screen personality with no business being in politics.
> Ronald Reagan
> Donald Trump

He's too polarizing.
> Ronald Reagan
> Barack Obama
> Donald Trump

He has very weak foreign policy.
> George Washington
> John F. Kennedy
> Jimmy Carter
> Barrack Obama

He doesn't think before he speaks and won't stick to the script.
> Ronald Reagan
> Donald Trump

He's leading us toward corruption.
> George Washington
> Bill Clinton
> Donald Trump

He's using the Presidency to enrich himself.
> George Washington
> Bill Clinton
> Donald Trump

That can't be his real hair!
> Ronald Reagan
> Donald Trump

He divides us, rather than unites us, and he fuels the fires of racism.
> Ronald Reagan
> Barack Obama
> Donald Trump

Everyone's a Critic

He's the worst President ever!
>Warren Harding
>Richard Nixon
>Jimmy Carter
>Ronald Reagan
>George W. Bush
>Barack Obama
>Donald Trump

He lied to the American people.
>John F. Kennedy
>Lyndon B. Johnson
>Richard Nixon
>Ronald Reagan
>Bill Clinton
>George H.W. Bush
>Barack Obama
>Donald Trump

Okay. I'm sure you figured it out very quickly. *All* the Presidents listed after each statement are the correct answers. They all got criticized. Some of those criticisms held up historically. Some were just the typical hype that fades following campaigning or an administration's end.

We are very fortunate in the United States of America. Speaking out against the President is legal. It's protected in our right to free speech.

Very few people sit in positions where the better act of respect and historical decorum dictates restraint in criticizing the sitting President. Those people are our former Presidents. This is particularly true when a person is the immediate past-President. Traditionally, that individual is expected to not use the "wake" of their popularity to divide the people by criticizing their successor.

Naturally, during the campaign season, the gloves come off and they can campaign for whomever they choose. Following the election, however, they are expected to be part of the nation's "voice of reason" in aiding the peaceful transition of power.

It's long been held in this nation that no one should be intimidated into not speaking out against something they believe, even when it is the President. In a May, 1918 newspaper editorial, Theodore Roosevelt said that speaking out against criticism of the President "is not only unpatriotic and servile, but is morally treasonable to the American public." That's strong.

So, let's set politics aside and look at some of the actual accomplishments of some of our highly criticized Presidents. Then again, we don't all look at things the same way. What one person views as accomplishments, another may see as setbacks.

> *"Government is not the solution to our problems.*
> *Government is the problem."*
> -- President Ronald Reagan in his 1981 Inaugural Address

Richard Nixon re-opened relations with China, signed one of the first treaties that limited the nuclear arms race, created the Environmental Protection Agency, and was the first President to have achieved a balanced budget.

Once panned for not understanding foreign policy, President Jimmy Carter pushed for more human rights in our foreign policy, and he brokered the Israel-Egypt Peace Treaty. He also created the Department of Energy and the Department of Education.

Despite criticisms as a movie actor and a shoot-from-the-hip cowboy, President Ronald Reagan helped shatter the Cold War with Moscow and boosted nationwide optimism about our future. He also won re-election in the biggest landslide in history, stood up to iron-fisted union power, and shrunk government, returning many decision-making powers back to the states. His insistence on domestic spending restraint, across-the-board tax cuts, and deregulation launched an economic boom that created 16-million new jobs and lasted for two decades.

Everyone's a Critic

Under President Bill Clinton's leadership, we saw the lowest combination of unemployment in over two decades, a 5-day waiting period for handgun purchases went into effect, and the Direct Student Loan program helped more students attend college without having to pay for it until after they graduated. After his two terms in office, he left the nation with a balanced budget and a surplus, along with a record of creating 22-million new jobs.

George W. Bush created and lives in one of the "greenest" homes ever built, collecting & utilizing rain water, generating its own power, and utilizing solar energy, among other features. Living "green" advocate and avid critic of Bush's lack of environmental sense, former Vice-President Al Gore, on the other hand, was found to be living in a lavish personal estate consuming as much energy as a small community.

Interestingly, President George W. Bush established the largest underwater national park in the world. Papahānaumokuākea Marine National Monument, covering some 140,000 square miles around some uninhabited Hawaiian Islands, was established in 2006. Naysayers didn't have much to say about that. Ten years later, during the 100th anniversary of our National Parks Service, President Barack Obama extended the borders of most of that park out to the exclusive economic limit of 200 miles, quadrupling the total area included to over 580,000 square miles.

Often, Presidential criticism and many other "realities" are more a matter of perspective and perception. Consider the following example.

People for the Ethical Treatment of Animals or PETA is the world's largest organization for animal rights, with more than 6 million members. They advise supporters with the best tips for taking photographs at a demonstration.

That is smart thinking. I remember seeing a PETA demonstration in New York City a number of years ago. One videographer took an establishing wide shot, revealing a handful of protestors chanting and picketing as New Yorkers walked past, unabashedly ignoring the event. One videographer took several shots that captured the emotion with close-ups of passionately angry protestors' faces, slogans on their signs, and a concerned expression of a passer-by.

Now, depending on which video a viewer saw, perception of the event would be entirely different. The first video made the effort look small, detached, and ineffective. The second made it come across as powerful, meaningful, and passionate.

There we go. Perception becomes reality, not to be confused with actuality or facts. Perception clouds what's truly happening and "becomes" our idea of fact. While not 100% inaccurate, it's slanted.

Here's another story. I watched and listened as a man, who happened to be Black, related on video via social media what had happened to him on one particularly blustery winter evening in NYC. He was down and out, on the brink of becoming homeless. He stumbled into one of the many shiny buildings on 5th Avenue. Instead of being kicked back out onto the street, a well-dressed businessman did the unthinkable. He listened to him. Then he hired him, saying, "Welcome to the family."

Boxer William Campudoni, who grew up without a father in Spanish Harlem, then worked for real estate mogul, Donald Trump, for many years, seeing him on good and bad days, through upturns and downturns in his life. As Donald Trump was campaigning to become President of the United States, Campudoni grew tired of hearing all the bogus accusations getting repeated again and again. He added that they couldn't be further from the truth. He said that though he never had a father, quote: "Donald Trump taught me to act like a champion."

That said, I doubt there are many who would argue that, as a person, President Trump can come across as "rough around the edges." He often expresses little regard for politeness. He seems to have no "filters." If he thinks it, he says it. Or he tweets it.

Everyone's a Critic

I say, "comes across" with all deliberateness, as I do not know him. So, what I can reflect is what I perceive. In a twist that seems all too common, those who *do* know Donald Trump may well feel discomfort in the way he expresses without filters. However, I can't help but notice that everyone who truly knows him says the most wonderful things about him. They talk of his unadulterated integrity, his blatant honesty, his depths of kindness, and his straight-out compassion, especially for the underdog.

When he first began his run for the White House, most political insiders smiled, giving very little credence to his chances. As it became clearer that he was a force to be reckoned with, we started hearing a tirade of negativity. One of the big ones that's been repeated a *lot* is that Donald Trump is a wretched racist.

Every time we turned around it seemed that someone was saying, "Donald Trump is a racist." Hillary Clinton even said it during her 2016 campaign, so it must be true, right? I mean, the Clintons and Trumps were friends. They'd even attended Donald Trump's wedding to Melania.

Remember that just before the election, Hillary Clinton said that she was, "sick and tired of the negative, dark, divisive, dangerous vision and behavior of people who support Donald Trump." Well, if you'll pardon the expression, this certainly smacks of the pot calling the kettle black. Her campaign struggles had seemed much ado about negativity and divisiveness.

Think back. Donald Trump, the real estate tycoon, had been extremely popular in Hollywood inner circles. Everyone's darling. He'd even been honored with that star on Hollywood's Walk of Fame in 2007.

Then, as he drew closer and closer to securing the Republican nomination, never mind being elected President, his Hollywood cronies turned on him... detested him. Called him a racist. Called him a bigot.

Again, if friends say it, it must be true. Right? Or... did politics inspire a powerful need to create a public *perception* that Donald Trump is a complete creep?

In truth, people who are not driven to political odds with him tell multiple stories about Donald Trump that are at complete odds with the most insidious name-calling.

An unexpected groundswell of support arose from all corners of our country. Black community leaders started coming out publicly with statements about why they were not lining up with most Blacks and supporting Hillary Clinton or Bernie Sanders.

Celebrities, including some who'd been fired from his "Celebrity Apprentice" TV show more than once, broke ranks and hailed Trump for being a breath of fresh air, a great family man, and a totally honest person.

Everyday citizens, black and white, male and female, young and old, started openly talking about the fact that our nation hadn't had any big changes, regardless of who was President. Some passionate and well-spoken people from the black community started imploring fellow Blacks to support Donald Trump to give fellow African-Americans a chance to get better jobs, schools, opportunities, and safety.

Opponents openly laughed. They knew Donald Trump couldn't possibly get elected.

As weeks and months passed, and it became clear from attendance at his many rallies that he was indeed a force with which to be reckoned, tones changed. Donald Trump stopped being the sole target of criticism. The new bull's-eye landed on his supporters.

That meant that Americans were criticizing fellow Americans. If someone shared that they were voting for Donald Trump, they were scoffed at and labeled with words like ignorant, racist, bigot, Nazi, idiot, Marxist, stupid, and faggot.

When Hillary Clinton lumped Trump supporters into her "Basket of Deplorables," the labels resonated coast-to-coast. With just 60 days to go until the election, Hillary Clinton very well may have undone her own campaign in just that one speech. As we've mentioned, Trump supporters from all walks of life started coming out of the woodwork, proudly claiming to be "Deplorables."

But perceptions, fired by constant repetition, split our already divided nation even more.

I was personally saddened as I listened to conversations and read comments from people I knew to be intelligent, caring people. Insanity seemed to have taken over so many lives. The cause for the dramatic polarization was constantly touted as being Donald Trump.

In truth, the hate-speak did not come from him. I kept hearing angry words, dramatic accusations, fear mongering, inflammatory expressions… aimed *at* Donald Trump and, far more alarmingly, at his supporters.

The more candidate Trump talked about protecting Americans, stopping illegal immigration, enforcing existing laws, creating more jobs, rebuilding our infrastructure, fixing the health care insurance mess, and getting the economy growing again, the more media types called him a racist and bigot. The more he was labeled a racist and bigot, the more the public echoed the sentiments. The more the sentiments were echoed, the more they were believed. Perception became reality for millions of people.

Perception did not allow actuality to even be considered.

Okay. I remembered hearing the disappointment of Republicans following the election and re-election of Barack Obama. "Not my President." "How can Americans have been so gullible?" "This is bad news for America." Hmmm... the same fears we heard expressed by Democrats following the election of Donald Trump.

But folks seemed to get on board in 2008, rally together, and do what we typically do as Americans. We move forward. We work hard. We respect each other and our differences. We don't "go after" people for holding different political thinking than ours.

At least that *used* to be part of the American way... part of what made us positively different from some other parts of the world... parts that lack stability.

Now America welcomed a new President in Donald Trump. While millions expressed relief and positive hope for big changes, millions of others felt the pangs of disappointment. Many had wanted to see the first woman become President. Many had simply wanted to see anyone other than Donald Trump become President.

I had never seen such hatred, loathing, and anger spewing from so many corners of this nation. Anger seemed to seethe through every expression regarding America's President.

As we've detailed, people were attacked, bullied, and beaten for voting for Donald Trump. Protests turned ugly with people hurting people and destroying others' property.

While many perceived President Donald Trump as inspiring hatred, this daunting show of *counter*-hatred completely overshadowed even the most vehement perceptions of Donald Trump or his supporters.

These were not just my perceptions becoming reality. These expressions reflected actuality. A hate-filled and angry America had arrived. The racial unrest and class warfare that surfaced early in Barack Obama's Presidency now appeared in full bloom.

Everyone's a Critic

On February 1, 2017, just days after Donald Trump's inauguration as President of the United States, CNN convened and aired a panel that stated, "Donald Trump doesn't care about black people."

They even did it with a straight face. Ludicrous. Mortifying.

President Trump is not relying on "dependency policies" and wants to get rid of the misguided thinking to "have a child and get a check." This does not make him against Blacks. Quite the opposite. "Have a child and get a check" teaches people of every color to be dependent and not independent, and it perpetuates complete government dependence for the next generation. Ugh.

Further, let's look at another fact. Historically black colleges had spent years begging President Obama to allocate funds to help them. He didn't do it. On July 3, 2017 it came out that President Donald Trump had done it in his first 30 days.

Sorry, CNN, but that doesn't sound like a President who doesn't care about black people. Hmmm... I don't recall CNN or anyone else making a big to-do about President Trump having done in 30 days what President Obama failed to do in 8 years.

I believe we all need to take steps to put racism in its proper place... in the annals of history. Unfortunately, many people inadvertently continue to stoke the flames instead. Take the 2-man comedy team of Arceneaux and Mitchell, for example. They noted, "What with all the cotton black people picked during slavery, seems like we should be able to walk in the mall, and anything that's 100% cotton, we ought to get for free."

I get it that both Curtis Arceneaux and Norman Mitchell likely have ancestors who were slaves in America. That said, because slavery existed for many generations all around the world, most people of any race may also have ancestors who were enslaved. So, I get the social humor and even the twist for retribution.

On the other hand, I also get the fact that no Blacks in America today have ever been slaves, just as no Whites in America have ever been slave owners. So, why should Blacks today, even in jest, suggest they are owed something from the rest of us? If a white man or woman today works to make a living, should a black man or woman be entitled to some part of that money or the goods the other person produced? I do not think so.

Yes, indeed, slavery is a horrible part of man's inhumanity to man. Unfortunately, even though it's outlawed virtually everywhere, it continues to go on in places. Look at the sex slave trade or the millions who work for almost nothing in far too many countries. They are enslaved every bit as much as the slaves bought and sold around the world during the time of slavery in America... and even our indentured worker force that brought millions of immigrants to this country.

I believe we, as a nation, owe all people an opportunity. What we each do with that opportunity is up to each of us.

It's not been easy for any peoples to break out of bondages of all sorts. However, it's also true that millions have done just that. They've broken the patterns, gone against the grain, and worked hard, never expecting handouts. They've sacrificed in order to create an even greater opportunity for the next generation. That's how most of our ancestors believed and behaved.

Tip: Let's not just criticize whatever people or forces seem to be holding us down. Let's look at obstacles, indignities, and injustices, not as excuses to "stay down," but as stepping stones and building blocks... reasons to do even better.

24
Personal Rights and Responsibility

"You fail all the time. But you aren't a failure
until you start blaming someone else."
-- Bum Phillips (1923 – 2013)
NFL Coach

We are happiest when we don't respond to road rage or pity party invitations. This goes double for the negative garbage someone spews on social media. Resisting the urge to reply takes discipline. However, unless we simply love the fight, it's healthier to not get caught up in it.

We each get to decide how we use social media... spreading mayhem or being an optimistic voice of support. Whatever we choose, it's most important to not seek somebody to blame.

Another hot button issue comes to mind when we talk about personal rights and responsibility. That is the case for gun control. Even responsible gun owners don't want weapons in the hands of the wrong people. That's why waiting periods are important... both for background checks and to build in a cooling off period in case someone is off balance or very angry.

Perhaps it's time we make the case for anger control instead. We are all tired of turning on the news only to learn there's been another horrific example of man's inhumanity to man. Then we listen through all the hand-wringing and investigation as officials and politicians try to figure out how it could have been prevented and find someone to blame.

Whatever happened to personal responsibility? I am to blame if I lose my temper. We all are. We each need to take personal responsibility for our anger control... or our lack of anger control.

If we remove the guns, criminals will still have them. The same goes for anyone who wishes to do harm to others. So, all we would succeed in doing is removing the guns from law-abiding citizens.

And the elite, because if you know the right people, you'd get exceptions. As we've said, this was a basic reality during the time of the U.S.S.R.

As much as I can see the benefits of restricting certain classes of weapons, I also see the actuality. Anyone bent on destroying others will do so, regardless of the laws.

It's true. Knives kill more people than guns. Yet, we all have knives in our homes, and there is no one screaming for better knife control laws.

Anger control. We can't legislate it. It must start with each individual person.

Personal responsibility. That also must be taught. However, as a society, we all would benefit if officials stopped trying to make excuses for people when they have done evil. We look for someone else to blame. We turn assailants into victims of circumstance.

Don't buy it. Don't even rent it. We are all responsible for our actions, especially when we choose poorly.

I grew up in a time when automobiles did not come with seatbelts. Now it would be illegal to make such a car. And many states have laws requiring drivers and passengers to wear those seatbelts.

This initially started with requirements for underage passengers to wear seatbelts. Okay, I get that. Children cannot make safety decisions for themselves. The adults had the personal right to choose. That right has all but disappeared. We can still choose to ignore the law, but we risk getting fined.

It's the same as when we ignore speed limits. We have the personal right to follow our free will and break laws. Funny how we get ticked off when we get caught.

Helmet laws developed with some controversy. Motorcycle riders used to be able to choose how they wanted to ride and whether or not they wore a helmet. Now many states require helmets. Bikers have lost their personal right to choose.

"But wait," we may say. "These laws are for people's safety." So, we want government to legislate our safety?

The argument *for* much of this stemmed from what happens when there are crashes. If someone lives but is badly injured, it's a very expensive process to help people recover. Other people ultimately ended up footing many of these bills. Our personal choices and personal responsibilities take a back seat.

As we've discussed, the National Anthem took center stage in 2016 as NFL player Colin Kapernick's personal statement against racial and social injustice. First, he sat it out, refusing to stand as is the custom. Though I found it unseemly, it merely reflected on him. However, it struck me as peculiar coming at a time in our U.S. history in which we had our first black president.

Most likely, I found this protest choice peculiar because of my own upbringing. Whether we were listening to a baseball game on a radio in the backyard or watching an event in person, we learned that we should be on our feet by the time the third note of the National Anthem was played. We learned in school that this showed respect for our nation, our freedoms, our unique American opportunities, and the enormous number of people who had served in our military to keep our rights intact.

That said, I can't begin to know what it was like to grow up Black in a White-dominated America. Nor can a man have any idea what it was like to grow up female in a male-dominated America. Regardless, I find myself choosing to look at our commonalities.

This is a land of opportunity. I am "Blue-Collar Cathy." I believe in working hard, though there are no guarantees of success.

Also, I don't believe that kneeling rather than standing for the National Anthem is exercising our "right to free *speech*." We talked about this in Chapter 2. When NFL athletes protested, they alienated fans and supporters because they were doing this at their jobs... their rather super jobs. They'd have likely had a completely different and non-divisive public reaction had they chosen to make their statements in some other venue. Highly-paid athletes using the National Anthem at the start of NFL games for their "quiet protest" is not impressive.

On the other hand, I cannot say that I am impressed when our nation's President gets involved in issues that I see as outside the Executive Branch of our national politics either. It matters little whether I agree with them or not. I am just not enthralled.

Remember when President Barack Obama came out with statements regarding a black person being killed by a white police officer? Each time, it stirred public sentiments against our first responders. He also fanned the flames of racism in this nation when he failed to make *any* statement when a black person killed a police officer. This sort of behavior smacks of racism and alienates people. It's nothing more and nothing less than divisive.

President Obama helped turn a local incident into a national crisis, seemingly urging people to hate the police.

Then came President Donald Trump coming out with statements regarding NFL football players refusing to stand during the National Anthem. I happened to agree with his opinion, but tweets and retweets only fanned the flames of racism... again. Players were pitted against players. Fans against fans. Fans against players.

Then, as New England Patriots owner, Robert Kraft, tweeted, "There is no greater unifier in this country than sports and, unfortunately, nothing more divisive than politics."

Personal Rights and Responsibility

As I watched the start of the Patriots game on one Sunday, I found myself respecting the CBS broadcast team. Directors did not focus the cameras on the players kneeling in protest beyond a couple shots. Thank you. That's fine. Tens of thousands of people were standing, hands on hearts, and voices raised in song.

Well, the players have a right to kneel, whether we are forced to pay attention or not. They also have the right to stop accepting their multi-million-dollar U.S. salaries. They have the right to move to a nation that never had racial or social injustice.

Oh, that's right. No such nation exists. They may have to try the moon. Yup, that's sarcastic, but despite our great many imperfections, I still believe the U.S.A. is arguably the greatest nation on earth.

We do have the personal right to peaceful protest. We have the right to counter protest when someone's position is opposite our own. We also have the right to ignore those with whom we disagree.

Women have faced great injustices for many generations. This is not an American issue. This is a world issue. Bra-burning protests in the 1960's reflected the sentiments of protest.

> *"Women share with men the need for personal success,*
> *even the taste for power,*
> *and no longer are we willing to satisfy those needs*
> *through the achievements of surrogates,*
> *whether husbands, children, or merely role models."*
> -- Elizabeth Dole (1936 -)
> Former United States Senator

Even today, a great many males resent females in their workplaces. Worse yet, we still hear outlandish criticisms bantered about regarding women. There is no logic. There is merely some foolishly outdated fraternal bonding going on... among what I call the Testosterone Toddlers.

The Bimbo Has *MORE* Brains

"We've got a generation now who were born with semi-equality.
They don't know how it was before, so they think, this isn't too bad.
We're working. We have our attache' cases and our three-piece suits.
I get very disgusted with the younger generation of women.
We had a torch to pass, and they are just sitting there.
They don't realize it can be taken away.
Things are going to have to get worse
before they join in fighting the battle."
-- Erma Bombeck (1927 – 1996)
American Humorist

I heard those words by Erma Bombeck. I recognized them as a sign of our complacency.

Whether we are talking about seatbelt laws or gun control, racism or women's rights, none of us should be complacent. We humans are slow to evolve. We each must do our part. We show far more logic and reason when we take personal responsibility and stop passing the buck.

However, we shouldn't pat ourselves on the back for calling attention to an issue of importance unless we are also acting to improve that situation. Thus, protests such as kneeling during the National Anthem to protest police brutality and racism or wearing a black dress to the 2018 Golden Globe Awards to call attention to Hollywood's rampant sexual misconduct should only be a starting point. Then I want to see those participating in the protests participate actively and positively in their communities. *That's* taking personal responsibility. I adore athletes and other stars who do.

Tip:
"I look at myself as a product of my choices,
not a victim of my circumstances."
--Kellyanne Conway (1967 -)
Counselor to the 45th President of the United States

25
The Rules Don't Apply

What's good for the gander is good for the goose. Right? Some households, companies, and even countries do not seem to "get" that fact.

We could be living in a home where one spouse feels entitled to socialize when, where, and with whom they please. Yet, if the other spouse meets up with a friend for lunch or sees family, it is not understood, appreciated, or sometimes even tolerated.

Or we may work in an environment where a couple of people on the same schedule as we are seen to come and go as they please. A child of theirs has a sports event or practice or dance class or birthday party or some appointment. This employee regularly arrives to work late by an hour or more and frequently departs an hour or two early. When some other family member is ill, this employee takes days off to assist.

This is all good and fine. Family first. That is why employers offer personal time as a benefit... or medical time or vacation time. Some people use personal time allowances for vacations. Others use it for day-to-day lifestyle needs, often having to forego vacation time off, because they have used up all their earned time for daily needs.

The "bee in my bonnet" gets stirred up when certain employees meet their day-to-day time off needs without deducting any of their medical or vacation or personal time allotment. Yet, when most employees need to have an afternoon or morning free, they must follow the rules and use their time off benefits.

When the offending employee is at the same pay level as we are, such inconsistencies can get old really fast. It can become very frustrating to be exercising personal and professional responsibility when others around you are not and are getting away with it.

Now, when it comes to nations pulling this "different strokes for different folks" attitude, the abuse negatively affects the entire society. It may be as obvious as what the Soviets called "the Intelligentsia." Remember, this is that upper layer of the so-called equal society. They are the "correctly-connected" people, politically. They have personal wealth. They have celebrity. It means societal rules don't apply, certainly not equally.

For example, in the previous chapter I noted that in the U.S.S.R. private gun ownership was against the law. Yet, we'd see some lovely homes with guns proudly mounted on a wall or over a fireplace. Recall that the wait time for a Moscow apartment was some 20 years. Yet, we met a young family with an apartment that was not shared with other relatives, which was the absolute norm at the time.

Such realities as these were instant indicators that the person or people were in that silently-privileged class.

Then there are the nations with violently oppressive conditions, particularly if you are female or gay. Women must keep their heads, faces, and bodies covered and cannot come and go as they please. They must be accompanied out of their homes by a male family member. They must not work outside their homes.

Some of these cultures think their daughters have totally dishonored their families if they even try to date someone from a different sect of their same faith. And they think it's honorable to murder these girls… in the name of honor, of course.

There are also cultures that want to be sure "their women" never can enjoy sex. They literally cut out the entire clitoris, and often the surrounding area when the girl first becomes a young lady.

Of course, no such rules apply to men in these societies.

The Rules Don't Apply

Remember, we should be careful when criticizing these societies, as if we were so much better. In truth, we don't have to look outside our own nation and history to also find differing principles applying to our citizens.

Women were always considered second class. Women could not vote. Women could not serve on juries.

As recently as the 1970's, women could not select a number of majors or fields of study at various universities. Several universities maintained different rules for male and female students well into the 1980's. Some of these included the right to live off campus or have opposite sex visitors in dorm rooms. Some female dormitories mandated enforced curfews, while male dorms did not. Such lists go on and on.

As with virtually all nations in the world, the U.S.A. had slavery, using and abusing people who had been literally hunted, captured, and stolen from their families, homes, and communities. Whether a slave was used for house duties or for hard labor matters little. Conditions were most often vile, at best.

Most slave owners considered their slaves to be property, not people. What on this earth ever makes any person think for even one minute that they have the right to buy or sell human beings in the first place?

This heinous practice has gone on for many centuries all around the world. However, our focus is on the United States of America.

Even after slavery was abolished, prejudice against Blacks made equal rights attainment a farce for decades. I will say one thing on the positive side. The U.S.A. was the first nation to not only abolish slavery, but to also deal with the struggle for equal rights on a *huge* scale and in multiple public forums.

Unfortunately, we humans tend to stick within our comfort zones. This is true for all of us, general speaking. So, when Italians immigrated here, they joined Italian neighborhoods. Irish gravitated to Irish areas. French Canadian, Chinese, Armenians, Dutch, Spanish… we all tend to do this. While the cultural familiarities can be good and supportive, especially in times of transition, this also presents economic challenges and language barriers.

Several cultures suffered a full generation of educational setbacks, because only the "mother tongue" was spoken in their homes, slowing children's advancement in American schools. In other cases, youth was encouraged to do what the family had always done, even when such trades, crafts, or skills would not help them advance more readily in America.

We also observe, especially in some primarily black sections of large cities, another ongoing struggle. This one deals with the perpetration of embroiling successive generations in tremendous anger, frustration, and resentment of slavery's injustices.

I get it. I had family members raped and murdered by marauding Turks. My family exists only because one tough lady disguised her two youngest boys as little girls, grabbed each by a hand, and ran away, escaping to Russia over Mount Ararat from sword-wielding Turkish soldiers Hell-bent on killing all Armenians.

Once in America they made the decision to become Americans. Did they like or trust anyone who was Turkish or represented anything Turkish. Nope. However, they did not pass on to us the need to endure their pain and suffering. They just wanted us to remember it and learn from it. They raised their children to speak English, to be strong, to get educated, to work hard, to endure, to succeed, and to be fair. They did not raise us to hate Turks or Turkey.

So, here we are in America… a generation later. I grew up in a home and community that did not "teach" us to be prejudiced. Everyone's story or background was unique. Often, the similarities included struggles and great pain at some point in a family's background. Yet the families persevered and taught love and tolerance to the next generation.

Still, as we have painfully observed during the last five or six years, a cavernous racial divide has been widening. Racism increasingly became a contentious issue that needed addressing. Yet, attempts seem to be increasing to make racism merely reflect white injustices against the black community.

By 2012, class warfare had somehow become "cool." And some very wealthy, privileged individuals had cleverly finagled themselves to be perceived as champions of the poor. Regardless, the "Have Nots" have been increasingly pitted against the "Haves." While I have not had monetary wealth, I have felt blessed to live in a nation where the abundant opportunities and possibilities flourish.

Black lives matter. White lives matter. Blue lives matter. Rich lives matter. Poor lives matter. Hello! *All* lives matter. No one group has a monopoly on this.

What sickens me the most is watching utter disrespect for others become a matter of course anytime people are upset, hurt, angry, frightened, or even concerned about something that has happened. This only perpetuates and enlarges the very environment of hatred that they are trying to protest.

Showing disrespect to someone we believe has shown disrespect teaches disrespect.

Showing hatred to someone we believe has shown hatred teaches hatred. Engaging in violence against someone we believe has engaged in violence teaches others to engage in violence.

Tip:
The viciously destructive cycle doesn't end until we *each* and *all* cease and desist in spewing negative at each other.

26
Greater Tomorrows

"The person that loses their conscience has nothing left worth keeping."
-- Izaak Walton (1594 – 1683)
English Writer

I think we agree on more things than we realize. Regardless of political party preferences, I believe we recognize the difference in supporting people who *cannot* work due to age, disability, or illness versus people who *will* not work due to inconvenience, job undesirability, a child at home, or laziness. I know we all recognize and agree on what is wrong and what is right. There's not a doubt in my mind that all voters want to see our children get good educations, our elders cared for respectfully, employers treat workers fairly, our military personnel and families rewarded for their service and sacrifice, etc., etc., etc.

We are bound by our morality and our hope. We are driven by our work ethic and our spirit. We are inspired by our passions and compassions. Together, all of us who agree and who disagree, work to accomplish progress.

"Without passion, you don't have energy.
Without energy, you have nothing."
--Donald J. Trump (1946 -)
45th President of the United States

When it comes to our own personal morals, we'll always find it easiest to maintain integrity if we do not operate in a gray area. We need to stick to the facts; we mustn't bend reality to rationalize bad choices or actions.

While working in television news, I recall scanning the scripts my co-anchor was to read on air. I always tried to do this to know what was going on and to avoid a blind read if suddenly I was asked to deliver that story on air. On one night I saw a story entitled "Jones No Show" (Jones is a contrived name I'm using, not the actual person's name.) It caught my attention because I had been slated to moderate a Congressional debate between Mr. Jones and Mr. Walker (also a fictitious name) on that very same day. The news script detailed how Mr. Jones had not even shown up at the debate site and left Mr. Walker dangling in an uncomfortable situation. Mr. Walker had "rallied" and turned a bad deal into a winner, however, by doing a full question and answer forum with the students at the hosting school.

Reality Check: A full three weeks before this debate, I had received telephone calls from *both* candidates to inform me that the debate had been cancelled. So, reading this news script came as quite a surprise.

Naturally, thinking it was an innocent mistake, I brought the matter to the news producer's attention. He looked quizzical, and then he took my information to management. In a few minutes the producer sheepishly approached my desk and said that it was out of his hands; the story was to read as written.

My co-anchor looked at me wide-eyed, because he now also knew that it was fabricated to make one candidate look bad. It's what we now might call "fake news." (Thank you, President Trump.)

After the producer walked away, my co-anchor asked me what he should do.

I said, "You heard the producer. Read the story as written."

Then I immediately rewrote the story with the truth. The facts. He was nervous that we'd get fired. I reminded him that he would merely be reading a script as it was written; I was the one sticking my neck out. He openly wondered why I'd do that.

It's that "no gray area" thing. I operate in black and white, fact or fiction, reality or fantasy. If they wanted to fire me for being honest and truthful, so be it. But my head would go on my pillow comfortably at night. I had not been raised to compromise scruples over someone else's warped political agenda.

The Bimbo Has Brains

By the way, we never heard a single mention of that rewritten story.

Success is more about how we feel inside than it is about the money inside our wallets. Though I think it would be lovely to not endure financial pressures, I want to be most rich with friendships and family ties, flush with marvelous experiences and adventures, and overflowing with good will and glad tidings. I want to leave people with more hope and self-belief than when we met.

Just a few years ago, I heard a young lady put it very well when she spoke at her Manchester Community College graduation.
Jacqueline Champagne, the Student Senate President, simply stated, "They never forget how you made them feel." Well said.

The commencement speaker at the same ceremony at Saint Anselm College on May 23, 2012, also made a great comment. Major David A. Fink, of the Army National Guard said, "Be brief. Be brilliant. Be gone."

In just a few words, they, knowingly or not, delivered words of wisdom that can help us all have greater tomorrows. They spoke of value. They spoke words that reflected respect.

While our community leaders, both the seasoned and the emerging, speak of such beliefs, I have faith in our nation.

I believe in the goodness of people. I see it in action every day as people volunteer for causes and organizations in which they believe. Whether it is for your Church, a favorite civic group, such as Kiwanis, or a charity like Easter Seals, give from the heart.

Whether you can give money, time, or both, give happily and give generously whenever possible. This is how we pass it or play it forward. This is how we renew and enrich our communities and our lives.

"We make a living by what we get, but we make a life by what we give."
-- Sir Winston Churchill (1874 – 1965)
Prime Minister of the United Kingdom

When we allow ourselves to get all wrapped up in political correctness, we are paying an inordinate amount of attention to our sensitivity to someone's potential feelings, rather than the facts. If you mean no harm nor insult to anyone, do not allow someone else to redefine you or your intentions.

There are billions of people on the planet. That means there are billions of opinions, too.

We could be much happier if we learned to seek and offer tolerance and acceptance, rather than gag orders for what we don't like hearing.

I suggest we seek what helps us love life and appreciate life. We should love people and what we do. We should all strive to be trustworthy throughout challenges, calm under pressure, and thoughtful in the words we speak.

We can each play a more powerful role in growing greater tomorrows. We can laugh when someone else needs it most. We can offer love when someone feels alone. We can shine light into darkened corners. We can leave a legacy of genuinely contagious enthusiasm.

Tip:
Never give up on a dream just because of the time it will take to achieve it. The time will pass anyway.

ABOUT THE AUTHOR

Cathy Burnham Martin's first published work was at age 6, when an early poem won a town library contest. That was back when her parents refused to let her have the then-popular Chatty Cathy doll, stating that one chatty Cathy in the house was more than enough. Though poetry took a back seat, she has driven her writing and blabbing proficiencies along a highly eclectic career path through recruiting college students, corporate communications for a tele-communications company, television broadcasting as News anchor with an ABC affiliate, management for an award-winning PEG access station, and bank organizing as Investor Relations Officer and Senior Vice President of Marketing. An active board member and volunteer, she received Easter Seals' David P. Goodwin Lifetime Commitment Award.

This professional voiceover artist, corporate communications geek, musical actress, journalist, and dedicated foodie earned numerous awards as a television news anchor and business woman. She has written, produced, and hosted groundbreaking documentaries, TV specials, and news reports, from the Moscow Super Power Summit and the opening of the Berlin Wall to coverage of New Hampshire's First-in-the-Nation Presidential Primaries.

A born storyteller, Cathy is a business speaker, a member of the Actors Equity Association, and a media coach. A 20-year Professional Member of the National Speakers Association, she was dubbed "The Morale Booster" and continues speaking and coaching through SpeakEasy Corporate Communications.

Cathy Burnham Martin narrates her books as well as those of other authors. Audiobooks appear on such sites as Audible.com as well as from Amazon and iTunes. In addition to fiction and nonfiction books, Cathy writes articles for the **GoodLiving123.com** blog, where information on all her books can be found.

www.ingramcontent.com/pod-product-compliance
Lightning Source LLC
Chambersburg PA
CBHW052125270326
41930CB00012B/2762